The Fountain FOCUS:

Whatever Works!

A Classroom Management Approach for
Traditionally and Alternatively Certified Teachers

D. L. FOUNTAIN

PublishAmerica
Baltimore

MW00911051

© 2006 by D. L. Fountain.
All rights reserved. No part of this book may be reproduced, stored in a retrieval system or transmitted in any form or by any means without the prior written permission of the publishers, except by a reviewer who may quote brief passages in a review to be printed in a newspaper, magazine or journal.

First printing

At the specific preference of the author, PublishAmerica allowed this work to remain exactly as the author intended, verbatim, without editorial input.

ISBN: 1-4241-2376-3
PUBLISHED BY PUBLISHAMERICA, LLLP
www.publishamerica.com
Baltimore

Printed in the United States of America

I Was Their Teacher . . . Dedication

Dedicated to everyone pursuing a teaching career

It is difficult to know what to say
I worked in my classroom day after day
Children came and children went
I stood straight, gave hugs, and bent
I read many stories of Dr. Seuss
I tied many shoes that were loose
My students loved stories of my yellow dog
Everyone laughed when I said he was an old
Hundred-and-ten-pound bump on a log
I know that the best day of the week
It was Friday, the day of my treat
I spoke of family and weekend events
Sometimes the students and I laughed
Together and made no sense
I look at all of the children I've known
I look at how all of them have grown
I remember there were terrific times
And times of tears
I know that they will remember I was
Their teacher throughout the years!

D. L. Fountain

Introduction / Foreword

When I was studying at Duquesne University twenty years ago, I investigated a research program that was the first to study how elementary and secondary classroom teachers, in the Pittsburgh Public School District, started the school year, how they established their initial rapport with students, and got their classrooms off to a smooth start. There were a lot of opinions about what teachers should do. But no one had ever studied what teachers actually did in their classrooms.

From those initial observations and sixteen other studies, I learned a great deal about how effective teachers manage their learning environments. For example, they begin early to teach rules, procedures, consequences, rewards; they monitor students' academic work and behavior carefully; they are proactive in stopping misbehavior before it happens; they establish ways to provide students frequent feedback; they work at making their instruction clear.

Knowing how teachers succeed in traditional classrooms, plus, being a teacher, coordinator, dean of academics, principal, and directing the alternative teacher certification program for a college district, I learned how teachers succeed in more challenging and complex classroom settings over the last twenty years. I had to find out how teachers operated effectively in more traditional settings where the teacher is the center of the instructional activities and the main source of information besides the textbook. I wanted to understand how effective teachers managed classrooms in which many activities were going on at once where students were working cooperatively and where students learned to take responsibility for their own learning.

My teachers and I spent many hours every week observing in elementary, middle, and high school settings. The research revealed two very important items. First, I found that these teachers did many of the same things that teachers in traditional classrooms do, such as making expectations clear, teaching rules and procedures, providing feedback, and monitoring students' work. Second, they also went beyond to teaching the students how to work together in groups, how to take on different roles, including the teacher role, and how to plan their own timelines.

What the research helped me to understand was how a super teacher incorporates what any good teacher in a traditional classroom does, but moves beyond that! This is what I incorporated into the Fountain FOCUS Classroom Discipline Approach Book. I believe that this book will help beginning, veteran, traditionally and alternatively certified teachers alike with their classroom management dilemmas.

Find the FOCUS in your classroom…and it will be smooth sailing for the rest of the school year!

Table of Contents

Chapter 1

PATTERN, PROTOCOL, PERFORMANCE, AND PRAISE!

First of all, you accept the fact that you have enormous power to influence student behavior. Here's how you can help your students choose an affirmative, positive behavior instead of an unconstructive means of conduct.

I'll always remember Shawn. He usually came to class late, talked when I was instructing, got out of his seat whenever he wanted, and rarely turned in a good effort assignments. Whenever I tried to talk to him, he'd ask indignantly, "What did I do?" At some point in your teaching career, you've probably had a Shawn in your class, the student who tests and challenges you and causes you to ask yourself—What can I do to help this student be the best that he can be?

I discussed Shawn with my contemporaries, who suggested that I look inside my classroom to see if something was happening that influenced him to be difficult. The more I examined what was taking place in the classroom, the more I realized that I wanted to help Shawn make better behavioral choices. Over the last 20 years, I have developed a discipline program based on my experiences with students, on ideas I've exchanged with many teachers throughout different states and countries, and on the most recent theories and explorations on student behavior. I created, designed, and implemented the "4 P's of Discipline" or the "Fountain FOCUS Discipline Plan," which enables teachers to apply specific strategies to reach individual students.

One important tip to keep in mind is that students choose their behavior, and we have power to persuade—not control—their choices. The "positive change" begins with the teacher; we need to learn how to interact with students so they'll want to choose the most appropriate behavior and abide by the rules. Here's what you do:

CATEGORIZE THE STUDENT'S BEHAVIOR

Usually, students misbehave because they want something—to be the center of attention or to boss others around, for example. The first step in Fountain FOCUS Discipline Plan is to identify exactly what the student wants when he misbehaves. Generally, students misbehave to reach one of these four goals.

Getting Noticed: Some students choose misbehavior to get extra attention. They want to be center stage, so they distract teachers and classmates to gain spectators and special identification. Some usual behaviors include making noises, using unclean speech, and creating pointless interruptions for the duration of the class.

Influence: Some students want to be the person in charge—of them selves, the teacher, and sometimes the whole class. They want everything to be done their way. At the very least, they want to show others that "you can't shove me around." These students aren't likely to observe the classroom rules or whatever the teacher desires. They will confront and quarrel with teachers until they think they've had the "final word."

Retribution: Some students want to lash out at their teachers or classmates to get even for genuine or imagined hurts. Students may sometimes make threats of physical harm or get indirect physical revenge by flouting, damaging, or thieving. They also may try to maneuver you into feeling upset or responsible.

Evading Failure: Some students feel derisory because they believe they can't live up to their own, their family's, or their teacher's hope for them. To balance their act, they act in ways that make them emerge inadequate, by procrastinating, not implementing their work, or pretending to have a disability. These students hope that everyone will back off and leave them unaccompanied so they won't have to look at the fact that they aren't performing up to their potential.

Can the misbehaviors in the classroom really have one of these four goals? Of course not. No premise, no matter how absolute, applies to every circumstance. 100 percent of the time; yet these four goals can help you categorize the misbehaviors more than 90 percent of the time.

TREAT THESE MISBEHAVIORS DIRECTLY

After you have categorized the misbehavior, you'll want to choose definite interventions for dealing with that type of behavior. Give these strategies an attempt:

Getting Noticed:

- Give "the eye" so the student knows you mean business.
- Stand close to the student and continue your lesson.
- Distract the student by asking a direct question or using the student's name while continuing your lesson.
- Give specific praise to a nearby student who's on task.

Influence:

- Avoid direct confrontation by agreeing with the student or changing the subject.
- Acknowledge the student's power and state your actions: "You're right, I can't make you finish the math problems, but I'll be collecting the assignment at the end of the class."
- Change the activity, do something unexpected, or initiate another class discussion on a topic of interest.

- Use time-out by giving a choice: "You may sit quietly, keep your hands and feet to yourself, and complete the assignment, or you may go to time-out in Mr. Weber's room. You decide."

Retribution:

- Revoke a privilege, such as not allowing the student to use play equipment.
- Build a caring relationship by using affirmation statements that give the message: "You're okay, but your choice of behavior is not."
- Require the return, repair, or replacement of damaged objects.
- Involve school personnel or parents if necessary.

Evading Failure:

- Acknowledge the difficulty of the assigned task, but remind the student of past successes he had doing similar tasks.
- Modify instruction, and materials.
- Teach the student to say "I can" instead of "I can't" by recognizing achievements.
- Provide peer tutors or ask the student to help someone else, perhaps a younger student, to help build self-confidence.

OFFER SUPPORT AND ENCOURAGEMENT

The difficulty with many discipline programs is that they give teachers strategies for addressing misbehavior, but don't show them how to keep the misbehavior from persisting. The Fountain FOCUS Discipline Plan assumes that students will misbehave again if the strategies aren't accompanied by encouragement techniques that build self-esteem and fortify the student's inspiration to oblige and learn.

Supportive techniques are neither time-consuming nor complicated to learn. Commend to utilizing them on a daily basis and your students will feel like important members of the classroom. Strategies for encouraging students fall into three categories:

Competent: Students need to feel competent of finishing their work in a suitable method. How?

- Create an environment where it's okay to make mistakes.
- Build confidence by FOCUSing on improvement and on past successes.
- Make your learning objectives reachable for all students.

Unite: Students need to believe they can unite and develop positive relationships with teachers and classmates. How?

- Be accepting of all students, regardless of past misbehavior.
- Give attention by listening and showing interest in their activities outside of class.
- Show appreciation by praise or written notes.
- Use affirmation statements that are specific and enthusiastic about a student's good behavior or abilities.
- Build affectionate relationships with simple acts of kindness.

Donate: Students need to donate to the well being of the class so they feel like they make a difference. How?

- Involve them in maintaining the learning environment by holding class meetings.
- Ask for suggestions when decisions need to be made.
- Use cooperative learning groups frequently.
- Encourage peer tutoring.

Students feel fine about themselves—and about their capability to be successful in school—when they trust they're competent learners who can unite in constructive ways with classmates and teachers. They'll also feel good about themselves when they find ways to donate to the class and to the school. Keep in mind that supportive strategies not only avert misbehaviors but also are being used successfully as hostility and gang deterrence trials.

PRODUCING ALLIES ALONG THE WAY

The Fountain FOCUS Discipline Plan is a route that promotes teamwork and collaboration. Creating a strong partnership with students and parents is an indispensable part of the preparation to maintain a positive discipline program that works.

Start by creating partnerships with your students. One way to involve them is to get their help in developing a classroom code of performance. They'll be more engrossed in keeping and enforcing the system of rules because they helped develop them. Another tactic is to teach students about the three categories of support and encouragement (competent, unite, and donate) and help them find ways they can give confidence to their classmates and gain it themselves.

Set the stage for valuable parent partnerships. Have your school administrator request that parents attend a gathering to get their say on the writing of a code of conduct. When you consult with the parents about a predicament that you're having with their child, limit your complaints to three or four misbehaviors. Chat with the parents which intervention and supportive strategies you'll be using to help their child select a more positive behavior. Send an understandable communication that you want parents to partake in the disciplining of their children. Reminding parents "you can't continually do it alone" will get your support that you want and need.

Fountain FOCUS Ideas:

- Spend time chatting with students in the hall after class
- Ask students about life outside school.
- Eat in the cafeteria with the students occasionally.
- Invite students to share a snack with you in your classroom.
- Attend school athletic, musical, and theatrical events.
- Get involved in a community project with your students.
- Schedule individual conferences to let students know about their progress.
- Chaperone school events.

- Make bulletin boards that display student work.
- Send cards, messages, and homework to absent students.
- Express real interest in students' work or hobbies.
- Share your interests with your students.

To get the Message, students must be given the Message.

Chapter 2

STAYING FOCUSED WITH YOUR CLASS

The origin of the word *discipline* traces back to the word *disciple*, meaning to lead to a higher cause, or a person who believes in and helps disseminate the teachings of a master. Contemporary definitions of the word *discipline* include references to punishment, behavior training, correction, and rules. When school children are asked about discipline, visions of writing lines, staying after school, rules, and other control-centered ideas come to mind. The present perception of discipline has little to do with *leading* students, and discipline is perceived as *reprimand or enforcement.*

Music educators, for example, my friend Mary in Florida, she defines her classroom discipline approaches as a specific process of regulating student behavior through a stimulus and response network. It may include enforcing regulations, establishing punishments and consequences, and creating a reward system for students who comply with the teacher's directives. That model and a few others describe the basic tenants of behaviorism included in the Fountain FOCUS Discipline Approach Program.

Popular programs including Lee Canter's Assertive Discipline and the Fred Jones Management Program provides structured control systems for reducing student misbehavior. Behaviorist programs are the most common management strategies found in schools today and are also seriously taught by university psychology departments. Music student teachers have no difficulty in understanding reinforcement schedules, theories of motivation, concept formation, behavior modification, cooperative learning, social learning, student-centered curricula, and research, which counters behavioral research and practices. Many teachers, though, believe that students can be motivated to behave when the learning environment—materials, activities, climate, support, and encouragement—are interesting and worthwhile, not by applying a corroboration schedule or other synthetic program or tool.

Today's students have learned that altercation is *better* than compliance. Trendy culture does not teach teamwork and common appreciation. Modern culture is obsessed with agonies, defined as *ritualized resistance and deliberation.* This is detrimental, as confrontations erode the blend of connections and authority, which is vital to constructing communities in our classrooms and schools. The result is as if every day is with a substitute teacher who cannot manage the class and sustain order.

Traditional reward and punishment systems do not necessarily extinguish aggressive or confrontational behaviors. D. L. Fountain believes that reprimands teach about the use of control, but not about how or why to conduct yourself appropriately. She cites research that shows increases in negative behaviors when punishments are applied. Stay positive and FOCUSED!

A FOUNTAIN FOCUSED APPROACH

The Fountain FOCUS Classroom Discipline Approach has emerged as a middle ground between laissez faire and control centered methodologies. This classroom discipline approach forces teachers to examine the total classroom environment: prevention methods, establishment of positive relationships, amending unproductive student behavior, and FOCUSING on the psychological and academic needs of the student.

The Fountain FOCUS Classroom Discipline Approach recognizes that all students will not react to all environments or interventions in the same way. Therefore, anyone who adopts a single program, fad, or viewpoint is probably not reaching a huge crowd of students. Just as students have different learning styles, students will have unique responses to classroom management approaches. Therefore, the teacher must develop an approach that best meets the needs of their students.

Many music teachers view this with disbelief. When one examines the conventional role of conductors in a symphony orchestra, the lineage of authoritarianism is apparent. Some perceive music teachers as strong, confident directors who dictate their desires from the podium. In addition, music teachers often work with larger class sizes, especially performance classes that may number 80 students or more. They feel that any surrendering of teacher control will result in mayhem and disorder. The Fountain FOCUS Discipline Approach does not mean that music teachers have to give-up their teacher-centered classrooms. Teachers are encouraged to examine the total environment and find the solutions which best meet their students' needs.

CONSISTENT ROUTINES AND PROCEDURES

The start of the class period is imperative to capturing and maintaining student awareness. Unruly hallway crowds rouse bouts of bewilderment, apprehension, or exhilaration prior to students entering the room. Music students often come straight from physical education, recess, or lunch. Their power levels have amplified. Teachers need strategies for REFOCUSING their students' attention at the beginning of class.

As a daily routine, warm-up problems can be used. While I taught in New York, I would write a new problem or question on the smart board or overhead. As the students enter the room, they work cooperatively on finding a solution. For example, a music theory lesson could begin by writing a short chord progression on the board and asking students to compose a melody for it. Students are put "on-task" instantly; they are also working together. For this approach to be effective, the assignment or problem must be significant and meaningful to the students. It should also have noteworthy relevance to the content. Students always resent "empty busy work".

A procedure should also be established for the paperwork that takes place at the beginning of class. These might include attendance, lunch counts, homework submissions, detention reminders, announcements, and other such matters. Students need to know how and when these matters are handled, preventing needless interruptions later.

Ensemble directors commonly use this procedure: when the conductor steps onto the podium, all talking stops. Once taught, this procedure is transferred to performance situations. For teachers who are not podium-centered, they can select a signal that tells students to *Stop – Take Note and FOCUS*!

D. L. Fountain believes that students should practice the Fountain FOCUS Discipline Approach procedures. Over time, procedures may also need to be re-taught. These consistent procedures may lead to greater time efficiency, leaving less time for students to misbehave and get off task.

VOCAL OPINIONS

Vocal feedback is an essential part of the teaching progression. In order for students to learn and mature, teachers must offer information in order to aid and guide the students' development. Several New York veteran teachers cite inadequate specificity of feedback as an identified element of ineffective teaching. Whenever feedback is given, D. L. Fountain believes that teachers should FOCUS on specific behavioral procedures which students can do to correct the circumstances. When students act up, D. L. Fountain recommends that vocal opinions should be specific, giving students information they need to keep it together.

In contrast, expressive feedback is a technique for making non-judgmental evaluations of student work or behaviors. Instead of praising or criticizing, the teacher describes what the student has presented. A percussion teacher might say that your expression is obvious and pointed, and your tone quality is thin and unproven.

ANTICIPATIONS, EXPECTATIONS, AND REACTIONS

Disruptions can occur, and teachers must plan their reactions. Students should be assigned chores such as memorizing measures from a song or numbering measures in their parts. These responses must be deliberate and planned in advance, as teachers must strive for stability and fairness in their management of the classroom. Teachers must consider whether these tasks are inspiring, appealing, or significant.

Positive teacher-student relationships are also important prevention. D. L. Fountain believes that successful band directors to be significantly higher in development of personal relationships and the need to accomplish tasks. Sincerity and conviction are the keys. Teachers who are contradictory, erratic, or irrational will have a difficult time earning the admiration of their students, often leading towards a boost in discipline troubles.

PLANNING FOR TEACHING ACHIEVEMENT

Most experienced teachers believe that preparation is an essential element of classroom management. Preparation elements may include short- and long-term lesson plans, organization of the environment, procurement of instructional materials, and anticipating student progress or problems. In performance-based courses such as band or choir, the key to teacher musicality is the synthesis and delivery of those elements into an expressive, meaningful, and worthwhile performance outcome. Good lesson planning and preparation should already account for musical readiness in relation to teaching the instructional unit. Simply knowing information about history or harmony does not necessarily equate with successful teaching. Delivery and structure will have a significant impact on student retention, motivation, and cooperation.

Assuming that planning and preparation are secure, music teachers should share their lesson plans at the beginning of each class. These can be in the form of a rehearsal agenda (so students can put their music in the correct order), behavioral objectives, daily goals, or other appropriate means. When students realize what is expected of them, their apprehension levels are reduced and accomplished FOCUS levels increase. As a result, they are less likely to act up because of insecurity. There are times, however, that despite the best planning, circumstances will disturb the flow of the lesson.

REFLECT BEFORE CONVERSING

Communication and awareness are collective actions. If we relate information with some person or item, we are more likely to maintain the relationship despite strong proof to disprove the correlation. When people read about someone who has been accused of a monstrous offense, we instantly connect that person with the crime. This occurs in spite of our sincere belief in blamelessness and impartiality. This prejudice can blur our ability to process information. Analogous examples can be found in the music classroom, as well.

For instance, music teachers are aware that some students do not practice their lessons outside of music class. If such a student approached the teacher for help with a solo, the teacher's bias may lead her/him to point the finger at the student of not practicing the solo when the student may have devoted excessive hours of practice time to the solo. Instead of concluding that the student needs further training or learning support, the teacher may inaccurately evaluate a need for increased practice time.

Students may also undergo message and perception errors. Students often misinterpret verbal and non-verbal communications from their teachers. For example, students often perceive the event of staying after school as a pessimistic reprimand. This is a learned perception because many teachers indeed use after school detentions as a punishment medium. Other teachers that I have taught with over the years teachers after school hours for helping students' progress, assisting highly-motivated students with extra projects, or to give individual attention to a student when the regular class meeting does not permit it. Students may also confuse the ordinary direction of don't talk in class with the self-centered belief of do not aid other students learn. Teachers often chastise students for talking in class, perceiving that the students are off-task and misbehaving. Sometimes that's true, but often they are talking about the subject matter. In instrumental music, students may be sharing information about fingerings or phrasing. Teachers should establish an environment in which students are encouraged to help one another learn while maintaining classroom order.

Perception and communication errors often cloud our aptitude to see the reality. Once a student is labeled as below average, not talented, or troublemaker, those relations bias the teacher to anticipate that trait from the student. All teachers must strive to eradicate these awareness errors from their classrooms. Throughout the course of months and years, students will grow and mature as a result of their experiences. Teachers must give students the flexibility to experience this natural development through encouragement and support.

CONCLUSION

Fountain FOCUS teachers can design their own classroom discipline approach which best serves the needs of their students. A variety of techniques, programs, and philosophies can be effectively employed. The classroom discipline approach is that—*a positive learning environment for all*—should guide teachers in managing their classrooms.

***Remember you are touching lives forever! Be Positive - Stay Positive! Start Right - End Right!!**

A Little Educational Humor...

Mr. Fountain: Joshua, why are you late?
Joshua: Because of the sign.
Mr. Fountain: What sign?
Joshua: The one that says, "School ahead, go slow."

Mrs. Donovan: Patrick, why are you doing your math sums on the floor?
Patrick: You told me not to do it with a table.

Mr. Ramirez: Matthew, can you name one important thing that was not here fifteen years ago?
Matthew: Me!

Mrs. Piel: Shelby, what is chemical formula for water?
Shelby: "H-I-J-K-L-M-N-O"
Mrs. Piel: Wait, what are talking about here?
Shelby: Yesterday, you said its H to O.

Mr. Saban: Jaycob, I told you to stand at the end of the line?
Jaycob: I tried, but there was someone already there!

Mrs. Dupont: Can anyone give me the name of a liquid that won't freeze?
Joey: Hot water!

Mr. Harris: Kacie, I said to draw a cow eating some grass but you have only drawn the cow?
Kacie: Yes, the cow ate all of the grass!

Chapter 3

16 FOCUS IDEAS!

FOCUS #1

A strategy that has worked well for me, if I have to speak to a student privately about his/her behavior, is to ask questions rather than lecture.

For example, "What do you think I'm going to say to you?" "Why do you think you are here?" "What kind of behavior do you think will assist you in getting the most out of this class?" And so on…I find that if I can elicit from the student what the problem is, she/he is more likely to pay attention to this "attitude adjustment". I usually wind up with, "What can I expect from you from now on?" The usual response becomes an informal contract and allows me to remind them of it in a very brief, but nevertheless effective, way in any future repetition of such behavior.

FOCUS #2

Give them short time limits—you may even want to use a stopwatch. "We are going to do this for 3 minutes. Go!" Then stop them and have them be completely quiet. At first, you will be mainly training them to "Stop" and "Go". They will be ready, and so will not be able to maintain "completely quiet" for very long. Sequencing is important. Wildest stuff just before the bell rings to send them somewhere else. But the very last thing I want to hear in my classroom is the humming of the fluorescent lights, which tells me that I have completely lost control because they are asleep or brain-dead. Might as well teach rocks to swim.

FOCUS #3

I learned this trick in an elementary cooperative learning workshop: When students are doing a speaking activity and you want to stop the activity and get their attention, raise your hand. Teach them to do 3 things when they see your hand raised. 1) stop talking immediately, 2) SILENTLY signal their partners to stop talking (without touching, shoving, hitting, etc.), and 3) raise their hand. You have stopped the activity without trying to yell over their voices. It also helps to give them a time limit—it keeps them on task. Hope it helps—it works with middle school and high school students, too.

FOCUS #4

Here's one idea from past years at the middle school. This may seem to reach back to elementary school, but if it works for you it could help. Teach the kids that when it is time to come back together you will give them a countdown and everyone will need to join in. You will put one hand in the air and call out the numbers from five to zero backwards in the target language (counting off by show of fingers). Students are to join in with you as soon as they catch on. At 'zero' there should be complete silence. Any student still talking could be required to do something (serious or light-hearted, you decide).

FOCUS #5

The beginning of the year is the best time to practice getting things started in a positive manner. Surely others on the list have some suggestions as well.

1. If you really need to "call roll", make it an active, productive thing—students must respond promptly with something that you have instructed them to say. This can be around a particular topic to review vocabulary, such as items of clothing or food; making it a rule that none can be repeated forces them to listen to those going before; requiring the article and giving an extra check/point to anyone who corrects a previous error also makes them listen.

2. This may be old-fashioned, but a seating chart prepared by the teacher still works! It breaks up the little cliques of friends who cluster together and want to chat. Intermingling carefully the boys and the girls also helps. It also means that you probably don't have to call roll, since an empty seat tells you immediately.

3. Over plan, with a variety of activities. Students who are busy doing productive work don't have the inclination (or at least the time) to act out.

4. At least the first time, make clear what the purpose of each activity is, so that they know how it will benefit them and support their learning. Otherwise they see some activities as just "busy work" and don't take them seriously.

FOCUS #6

On the high school side, a good classroom management trick to eliminate an unwanted behavior:

After the student has committed the behavior and has not ceased after being spoken to one-on-one, in class, indirectly, directly, and any other way possible, I ask the student to stay with me after school. When the student arrives, I give a sheet with three questions:

1. What behavior did you demonstrate in the classroom, which caused you to have detention here with me?

2. Why is this behavior unacceptable in this classroom?

3. What is your plan to improve your behavior? How can I help you to improve your behavior?

After the student answers the three questions, and we discuss each, then I inform the student that I will keep the writing on file for the remainder of the school year. If the problem persists, then we will call a conference with the student, student's parents, and myself to review the plan and make modifications to the plan.

FOCUS #7

My best advice is PREVENTION. Think through your lesson plans and try to minimize opportunities for misbehavior—pay particular attention to how you have structured student movement and transitions between activities. Try to alternate seat time with structured opportunities for moving about.

For everything else—I have found that humor is the key. Say it with a smile, empathize, and emphasize the fact that the student made a choice—you are not inflicting the punishment: I know how frustrating it is when one forgets things, but I'll bet you'll remember next time. I'm sorry that you chose to socialize instead of visiting the restroom, but I know that you can make it and that you'll remember to take care of your business first next time. (I don't give passes).

As to misbehavior—give the student a choice: You can either work quietly or sit here with me/in the hall. You can either stop punching Joshua or you can spend lunchtime with me. Make sure that you've thought through possible consequences in advance so that the choice you offer is one you can live with. Generate a list of possible consequences in your mind (or on paper) so that when a situation occurs, you are not caught off guard—you know exactly how you will handle it. Obviously, you have to "read" the situation and be somewhat flexible. However, just having a bag of tricks from which you can draw will make things much easier.

FOCUS #8

Of my 20 years in the education field, someone with a gun threatened me once when I worked at a school district in Florida. Obviously a lot depends upon your school and school district. We did have one incident in which a teacher was injured, so it does happen. But I found that being absolutely consistent, having clearly defined classroom rules and procedures and treating the students with respect (even when they didn't treat me the same way) kept me out of trouble.

The only time I ever felt unsafe was when my students were drunk or high on drugs. There was a certain amount of culture shock my first year, especially moving from Pennsylvania to Florida to teach in urban school districts. I got to know the kids and they knew I genuinely cared about them as people. Then, they were very respectful of me as a person.

If you want some specific guidelines and just a few personal stories, write me off-line. I loved my job and I loved my kids, and I taught plenty of gang members and drug dealers. We managed because somehow I convinced them to leave that outside their classroom.

FOCUS #9

Do we write these students off? No! Never! Of course not, because no matter how bad the class is as a whole, there is most likely at least one student that is learning, and more importantly, wants to learn. I don't mind preaching to the choir if that's where my spectators are. And who knows, the students on the periphery may learn something while they sit there and stare with their slack jaws and bored-to-tears expressions.

- Because we care.
- Because we want them to be happy.
- Because we want them to become productive citizens.
- Because it's our job to motivate them.

We shouldn't let ourselves be hurt by the reactions of an angry student. We shouldn't let their sorrow and anger and hurt at the world become our own. We shouldn't allow their anger to communicate itself, to infest others to gnaw at the social fabric of the classroom.

FOCUS #10

Do you know enough about your students' parents to have a sense of the kind of support you might expect from them? If so, I'd suggest a call home following this type of scenario:

1. Seek the aid of your disciplinary administrator by asking him/her to sit in on the phone conference call to a student's home.

2. During a time that you can access the student(s) have him/her/them report to you in the administrator's office.

3. Explain to the student that you are not pleased or comfortable with his/her behavior.

4. Hand him/her the phone and ask him/her to call one of his/her parents to explain why his/her French teacher would like to speak with the parent.

5. Once his/her explanation is given speak with the parent indicating specifics of the inappropriate behavior.

For a couple of years I was a Principal of a school in Texas. The students that I dealt with during those years really didn't like the "call home" or a "call to their parents at work!"

FOCUS #11

Hello gum chewers, I always did wonder what the big deal was about chewing gum??? Aren't there more important things to FOCUS on in the classroom? This is one of those "hot button" topics for me. Gum chewing would probably not be a problem if students knew how to discreetly chew without making snapping noises, playing with it, depositing it under seats when it is stale, and chewing with their mouth open. It is unsanitary, unsightly and obnoxious.

FOCUS #12

Some Fountain FOCUS Ideas for your classroom in the beginning of the year:

1. Walk and stand by one of the offending parties.

2. Stop talking. Make significant eye contact. Do not begin again until it is absolutely silent.

3. Never try to shout over student noise with directions or content.

4. Firmly tell students the expectation that, "When I'm talking, you are not. I am not able or willing to shout above noise." You can appeal to their sense of fairness, too. "Excuse me, but there's 30 of you and one of me." This can be a follow up to #2 if you feel it necessary.

5. Do not repeat directions a gazillion times. Do not answer questions from students who were talking while you were explaining an activity. There must be consequences for not listening when you are talking.

6. I have some students who feel that they are an exception to all rules and expectations. Sometimes I have to break it to them that nothing you could possibly be saying is more important than what I am teaching right now. This is real "tough love". Obviously, use with discretion.

FOCUS #13

- ☐ Posted rules, posted consequences.
- ☐ name = verbal warning
- ☐ name + 1 FOCUS POINT = (sentences or something else)
- ☐ name + 2 FOCUS POINTS = (more sentences or detention and/ or parental phone call)
- ☐ name + 3 FOCUS POINTS = (student is out of the learning environment)

*** OR *** TRY DOING THIS ANOTHER (WHATEVER WORKS) WAY:

Try putting names of students that are listening to you and following the class rules. Give them FOCUS POINTS for POSITIVE BEHAVIORS. I know that seems like a lot...and it is at first. But, if you have your class abiding by this POSITIVE (Fountain FOCUS) System, the second semester will be a breeze!! Try me, the class will almost run by itself!! It happened for me – it can happen for you!! Be Positive – Stay Positive!

I make the kids sign the backs of their index cards, that they fill out at the beginning of the year, that they have heard, read and understood my rules and agree to live by them. So when I have a parental conference regarding discipline it is all there—on the wall and a signature on file.

The main point is—writing names on the board is a silent, unobtrusive way to send a message. I am still teaching and did not let the motor mouth stop instruction. I have used this with middle school students and have used it successfully.

FOCUS #14

Other teachers have written with great suggestions for discipline, and I hope you will try some of them. However, I waited to see if anyone else would mention another important thing: You have to let your students see that you like them, and that you enjoy some of the things they do. (And you have to show it, even if you don't much right then.) The worst classes I've ever taught in 20 years of teaching middle school were when I started fighting with a class, and saw them as an enemy to be conquered—or at least a group to be controlled.

Guiding and leading your students work much better! Do NOT talk down to them. Treat them with respect, and most of them will respond with respect. Middle school kids are a real work in progress, and will have bad days—but they want to grow up, so it helps to treat them as if they are—as much as possible.

Try to enjoy them. Be interested in their lives out of school. Let them know you saw their name in the paper, or congratulate them on their play in the game. Change activities often. Be over-prepared. Try to do some active things to get them out of their seats at least once every day or two. Try activities that let non-academic kids shine: art projects, music . . . I've had kids make paper puppets and then use them to put on a skit. Some of the puppets were very creative. I have taught at almost every grade level in Pennsylvania, Florida, California, New York, and Texas, and I do prefer teaching the 4th – 8th grades. Intermediate and middle school kids are a challenge—but they really can be fun. Hang in there!

FOCUS #15

When I student-taught in the Pittsburgh Public Schools, I had two different cooperating teachers. One of them tolerated a lot more chaos than I could on any given day and the other didn't believe in background noise at all. (They were both excellent teachers, mind you.)

With one teacher, I was able to talk to her and explain my feelings. She was in the room a lot, but she was willing to "let go" enough to let me do what I thought I needed to. The other tried, but she just couldn't. She did let me do some things that she never would have tried, though. But, when I was evaluated, it was not good enough for her.

What am I saying?

Basically: talk to your cooperating or supervising teacher. That's the best advice I can give to any student/intern teacher. That's what they're there for – to help you figure it out!

FOCUS #16

When I taught in California, a new assistant principal instigated a innovative detention program. At one time detentions were served after school with designated teachers or with the teacher who gave the detention. The new system does not allow students any say in when they serve. As soon as a teacher turns in a detention form, the student is called in and must do some kind of service around the school during lunch. Usually they help out in the cafeteria, but they can also be seen outside picking up trash or in the halls scrubbing lockers. The consequence is immediate, and the loss of lunch—a time when they can be with friends—is a loss they really feel. Tardiness has dropped off to almost none.

In a New York school district where I worked, students were charged $5.00 for each tardy and $15.00 for each offense. They use this system at the local high school, but seem to have some problems with bringing it down to the middle school level. It does seem to be a problem that needs a school wide solution, and consistency on the part of all teachers in enforcing the rules.

Chapter 4

KEEP YOUR EXPECTATIONS HIGH!

The Fountain FOCUS Classroom Discipline Approach is an important requirement that demonstrates growth during your career. The purpose of the Fountain FOCUS Discipline Approach is to provide you with a "Whatever Works!" type of guide in managing your classroom and dealing with student behavior.

Children enter the world eager to learn, and they enter the classroom eager to learn as well. School is a place where all children should feel welcome. The classroom should be an inviting place where a student's mind can grow. School is a place where children mature, make life long friends, and make choices that influence them the rest of their lives. The learning atmosphere should be calm and welcoming.

I believe if one teaches in a positive learning environment with a positive attitude, students will have higher self-esteem and will be more productive. This can be done through bonding and interacting with the students. Having respect for each other also plays a role as well within the classroom. I believe within the classroom there should be rewards and consequences system. Students should be rewarded for behaving appropriately and punished for misbehaving. In order to help achieve this parents, students, and teachers should all be involved in the process of making rules and consequences for the classroom.

Teachers have a responsibility within the classroom to educate children to the best of their ability. Along with teaching, teachers also need to be able to manage the classroom and control the environment within it. Some of this management puts responsibility in the hands of the student as well. Students need to learn to manage their own behaviors, this is not something that is going to happen overnight, but with the right management plan it is possible. Management of a classroom and students is a big responsibility and with time and effort it can be accomplished to fit the needs of the students, teachers, and faculty.

We have all studied several theorist that have put their lives into helping teachers better their classrooms. Below is a list of the ten beliefs I relate with and anticipate using within my own classroom. There is also a few website links that you may use to find out more information on each particular theorist.

PROCEDURES AND ROUTINES

Beginning of the Day/ Attendance:

The beginning of the day is one of the most important times of the day. It sets out how your day is going to be run. When the students come into the classroom they should be greeted by the teacher, they will need to get out any homework or materials that were taken home the night before and place them on their desks. Then, they need to proceed to put their backpacks and jackets away in the cubby spaces, which have been labeled with their names. After the student has put away his/her belongings, they will need to move to the lunch count/attendance area. This is where they will place their stick by the appropriate lunch item, which they will be having that day. This is also how attendance will be taken as well. The teacher will need to check the lunch count/attendance area, to make sure everyone is accounted for. The teacher will then send the attendance and lunch count down to the office, which is usually done over the computer. The students then need to return to their seats and start their morning work; this will begin the morning quiet time. There will be some sort of morning worksheet or independent activity already placed on their desk, by the teacher. The students should work quietly on their morning work and wait for morning announcements. If the students finish their morning work, they are to read silently at their seats until announcements are finished. When students finish their morning work they are to place it in the basket labeled "Morning Work," unless otherwise instructed by the teacher. When announcements are finished the students will then wait for further instructions from the teacher.

Classroom helpers:

Classroom helpers play an essential role in the management of the classroom. These jobs help the teacher out tremendously and it gives the students some responsibility within the classroom as well. There will be a chart of weekly activities that each student will be in charge of doing. These jobs will rotate weekly so that every student gets a chance to do each job. Some of these jobs will include passing out papers, running errands, erasing the board, straightening books, mailbox organizer, washing desk tops, line leaders, and bathroom monitors. The teacher, at the beginning of the school year, will discuss each job in detail so every child has an idea of what each job will entail. The teacher will also be in charge of rotating the names each week, so that there is not any confusion among the students of who is doing which job.

Distributing materials/ Turning in student work:

The distribution of materials and turning in work can help a classroom run more smoothly, if the students know exactly how it will be done on a daily basis. Any materials (glue, scissors, markers, etc.) that are needed for the lesson will be distributed by the classroom helpers and/or by the teacher. These materials should be distributed after instructions are given, so the teacher can keep the attention of the students. If there is just a worksheet to be handed out, it may be distributed before the instructions are given.
When students are turning in finished work, they should place it in the appropriate basket. There will be a basket for each subject along with one for morning work. This is a way to help keep both the students and teacher organized throughout the day. Baskets also helps the teacher see who has not finished the work, without having to rummage through stacks papers in different subjects.

Transition to "specials":

While I was a teacher in Texas, our school called the fine arts time of the day "Specials." These periods are a time that the children look forward to during the day. This gives the students an opportunity to be outside of the classroom and feel more relaxed. This is also a time many teachers look forward to because it is usually their only break throughout the day. This gives the teacher a chance to get caught up on items that need to get done, such as grading papers and/or making phone calls.

When going to specials, students need to be lined up in two separate lines (boys and girls), which will be headed by the line leaders of the week. Before leaving the classroom the children need to make sure they have all the materials they need for that particular special, the teacher will most likely have to remind the students of this. Lines will also need to be quiet and straight before exiting the classroom. Student's will need to maintain their quiet and straight lines in the hallways of the school at all times. The teacher should walk the students to and from specials, and wait until the students are ready to enter the room before leaving. When the students are ready to be picked up the teacher should wait outside of the room until the "specials" teacher is finished with the lesson, then escort the students back to the classroom. The students will once again need to be in two straight and quiet lines in the hallways of the school.

Getting attention/ signaling for quiet:

Getting students attention can be a challenge, especially if the students are really excited about an event or if they are just being very talkative. It is important for the teacher to be able to get the students attention, in case there are instructions that need to be heard or if they are just getting too loud and out of hand. In order to get the students attention, I would use the count to five or lights off method. Where the teacher holds his/her hand in the air and starts out at zero and begins counting to five, raising a finger every so often. The students know that if all five fingers are up, then there is going to be a consequence and they better be quiet immediately unless they would like further consequences. The students that see the teachers hand go up, will put their hand up as well and begin counting with the teacher, in hopes of getting others attention as well. The consequence would be five minutes off recess for the entire class. If the disruption still continues the class will continue to loose five minutes of recess until they no longer have a recess that day. If the disruption is still occurring, the students will loose other privileges. This signal will be explained to the students within the first few days of school.

Emergency Drills:

Emergency drills are very important. These are thing that could happen at any given moment and the teacher needs to be prepared on what to do at all times. Emergency drills include thing like tornado, fire, earthquake, and hostage situation, act. At the beginning of the school year, the teacher should go over all emergency procedures, and review positions and procedures with the students so they will know what to do incase an emergency ever does occur. The teacher should also post all emergency procedures by the door to the classroom for further reference. If an emergency drill does occur the teacher should have a list of every student in the classroom for reference.

Dismissal:

Dismissal is another part of the day the students are looking forward to after a long day of hard work. At the end of the day, the teacher should review any homework the students have for the night and give any last minute reminders and answer any questions the students may have. Then have the students look around on the floor and have them pick up any trash that may be lying around and have them throw it away. When that is finished the students need to check their mailboxes and take home any papers in their mailboxes. Then, students need to get their backpacks and jackets from their cubbies and pack their bags to go home. Students then need to put up their chairs and line up at the door and wait patiently. The teacher will have flash cards to help the students review math facts before leaving for the day. When the student answers the problem correctly he/she is free to go.

Implementation of the Fountain FOCUS Discipline Approach:

The behavior of students in and out of the classroom reflects highly on the teacher and how he/she manages the classroom. It is important to have a set of rules or a code of conduct established for the students and the teacher within the first few days of school. The teacher, students, and parents should put these guidelines in place. Along with putting rules in place within the classroom there should also be consequences set into place if these rule were to broken.

Once these rules and consequences have been established they should be posted in the classroom for everyone to see and a note should be sent home to the parents telling them the rules and expectations that have been established within the classroom. This letter to the parents should be signed and returned, letting the teacher know that these rules have been acknowledged. There should also be a place where parents can give input to the rules and consequences set forth by the class. By giving the students and parents an opportunity to help set the rules and consequences within the classroom, I feel that there should be less confusion about what the expectations of the classroom are for the school year.

Once these rules have been set up within the classroom they will be enforced by a behavior board. The teacher must remember to check with the school for their discipline policy before introducing the class to the behavior board. This board will consist of a stop light with red, yellow, and green lights. Each light will be a different level of warning. The green light is the safety zone where all students will keep their cars when they are behaving correctly. The first warning will just be a verbal warning, but the next time the student is addressed for misbehaving they will need to move their car into the yellow light zone. The yellow light is the second warning; this is where the student has misbehaved after being given a verbal warning by the teacher or faculty. If the student has to move their car to the yellow light, they will loose five minutes of recess time or a privilege throughout the day. The third level, which is the red light, is the final warning. At this level the student will loose all of recess time and needs to have a conference with the teacher during recess. At this time the student will have a note sent home to the parents describing the misbehavior. The student will write this letter and the letter will be proofed by the teacher. If the student continues to misbehave, they will be sent directly to the principal's office. The teacher of the classroom will keep a daily record. At the end of the week, the teacher will give those students that have not had to move their cars a reward or an extra activity such as computer time for good behavior. I feel it is important to reward those students that have not misbehaved, but I also see it as an incentive for those who do misbehave, for wanting to do better.

Besides rules and maintaining them within the classroom, learning is the main thing that is to take place. In order to make sure that learning takes place within classroom the teacher needs to have a calm, collective, and positive attitude. The way in which a teacher presents themselves to the class has a direct effect on the way students act and learn within the classroom. If the teacher is upset about something or is having a bad day this is going to have a direct effect on the students learning. The teacher has to learn to set aside his/her feelings towards a situation and address the student's need to learn. I have always been told that attitude is the key to everything in life, and I truly believe this. I think with the right attitude about everything you do can make a difference.

It is also important for the teacher to model the behavior that is expected within the classroom as well. Keep your expectations HIGH!! I think it is also important for the teacher to be flexible; a teacher's day can change at any give moment, so it is important for teachers not to have their day set in stone. It is fine to have goals on what the teacher would like to cover during the school day, but do not rush to get everything in, just because it is on the agenda for the day. This will usually end up leading to teacher frustration and student failure. I think it is also very important that students engage themselves in social interaction and to have an active learning environment. This environment is basically in the hands of the teacher, and should be set up in a positive manner where all students can feel like they belong. It is important for teachers to assess students both informally and formally on daily to weekly basis. This helps the teacher stay in constant communication with the child's learning.

In order for a teacher to teach effectively throughout the day and address misbehaviors at the same time, the teacher needs to have short-term and long-term success goals. If a student is off-task, but not disruptive to the instruction or towards other students' learning, the teacher needs to continue with the lesson, but when the lesson is finished the teacher may want to call that student up to his/her desk and speak to them privately, by addressing the misbehavior and tell the student they need to get on task with the lesson. If off tasking continues the teacher may want to move the student closer to his/her desk, in order to keep the student from distracting other classmates.

If the student is off-task and being mildly disruptive to the teachers' instruction and other students' learning, the issue needs to be addressed immediately. In this case the other classmates are not listening to the teacher and the teacher is just going to end up frustrated by the end of the lesson. The teacher needs to address the class as a whole by telling them to put everything away and pay attention to the lesson being taught. Do not call the student out directly, but instead address the class as a whole. If the disruption occurs, give the class their first verbal warning and tell them that if the disruption occurs then cars will be moved. When the lesson if finished being taught the teacher may want to address the student personally and move them closer to the teacher's desk, so less disruption takes place.

If the student is off-task and seriously disruptive to the teachers' instruction or other students' learning, the teacher must address this misbehavior immediately before continuing with the lesson. This child should be give a verbal warning and told if addressed again, then the student will move their car. If the misbehavior still continues ask the student to move away from the group to a near by table and stay there for the remainder of the lesson. The teacher needs to speak to this student one on one and then move the students' desk away from the rest of the students, so there will be less chance for misbehavior.

If an immediate, serious threat to the physical safety of the teacher and /or students' occurs within the classroom, the teacher should stop everything and take care of the issue. First, either you or one of the students push the assistance button, which calls the office and ask for assistance in the classroom. The teacher must remember to remain calm during this situation, because if the students see you panicked, then it will only make them nervous as well. Then, when the assistance call has been made the teacher should address the situation in the best way that he/she knows how. If this misbehavior continues the teacher may wish to have the student(s) removed from the classroom.

It is also important that the teacher keeps track of misbehaviors by students within the classroom. This may become an important note if the child is ever diagnosed with a learning disability or disorder. It is so important for teachers to constantly reflect on their style of teaching and choices, so things that are not working can be changed to benefit both the teacher and the students. This is main part of the Fountain FOCUS Discipline Approach. Hope it works for you! If not, adapt this approach to your own teaching style!

I make mistakes so I can learn.
I learn so I can succeed.
I succeed so I can help others!

Chapter 5

CLASSROOM REWARDS: BRIBES OR INCENTIVES??

The word enticement is often used in education. Critics think that when we offer an incentive of some sort we are bribing our students. This is simply not the case. Webster's dictionary defines a bribe as " a gift or promise given unethically in return for a favor." We are not trying to persuade them to do something unlawful or dishonest. We are simply trying to amend their behavior in a positive manner. Of course, it would be nice if everyone was able to engage in academic activity and other appropriate behavior for the "love of learning," but the sad truth of the matter is that children sometimes have never experienced any success with academic work.

The goal of any behavior modification program is to wean the child or adult from the more obvious externally provided reinforcers to the intrinsic, more naturally occurring reinforcements that the successful completion of a task brings. The rewards are simply a means to show the child the intrinsic rewards that accompany the external rewards. Incentives, often confused with bribes by critics, are defined as something that incites to action; motivates; spurs. In the classroom, incentives come in the form of something that is preferred by an individual or an entire class.

> The Fountain FOCUS Classroom Discipline Approach suggests a system of rewards to motivate children to do their homework in a timely, acceptable fashion. D. L. Fountain would rather provide incentives to a kid and jump start the behavior, internal motivation and attitude change than watch kids fail.

In a perfect world, all students would follow the rules because it is the right thing to do. Unfortunately, in reality the ones that need incentives to help them see the intrinsic, more naturally occurring reinforcements that the successful completion of a task bring, outnumber those students.

While teaching fifth grade several years ago in Texas, my classroom was next to someone who used PAT on a regular basis. The students were allowed to earn time by exhibiting good behavior in the classroom. This particular teacher allowed them to bank time and use it every Friday afternoon. All afternoon. When used in that fashion, I think it loses the appeal. I believe that in order for it to be effective, it truly needs to be earned by the students. In my classroom I used incentives regularly with my students. They ranged from educational: spelling games, math puzzles and extra computer time, to simply fun: popcorn, class discussions, and the occasional movie (which was always tied to classroom reading).

THE RISKS OF REWARDS

Many educators are acutely conscious that reprimands and threats are counterproductive. Making children suffer in order to alter their future behavior can often obtain temporary compliance, but this tactic is unlikely to help children become ethical and empathetic decision makers. Punishment, even if referred to euphemistically as "consequences," tends to generate anger, defiance, and a desire for revenge. Moreover, it models the use of power rather than reason and ruptures the important relationship between adult and child.

Of those teachers and parents who make a point of not punishing children, a significant proportion turns instead to the use of rewards. The ways in which rewards are used, as well as the values that are considered important, differ among cultures. This digest, however, deals with typical practices in classrooms in the United States, where stickers and stars, A's and praise, awards and privileges, are routinely used to induce children to learn or comply with an adult's demands. As with punishments, the offer of rewards can elicit temporary compliance in many cases. Unfortunately, carrots turn out to be no more effective than sticks at helping children to become caring, responsible people or lifelong, self-directed learners.

REWARDS VS. GOOD VALUES

Studies over many years have found that behavior modification programs are rarely successful at producing lasting changes in attitudes or even behavior. When the rewards stop, people usually return to the way they acted before the program began. More disturbingly, researchers have recently discovered that children whose parents make frequent use of rewards tend to be less generous than their peers.

Indeed, extrinsic motivators do not alter the emotional or cognitive commitments that underlie behavior—at least not in a desirable direction. A child promised a treat for learning or acting responsibly has been given every reason to stop doing so when there is no longer a reward to be gained.

Research and logic suggest that punishment and rewards are not really opposites, but two sides of the same coin. Both strategies amount to ways of trying to manipulate someone's behavior—in one case, prompting the question, "What do they want me to do, and what happens to me if I don't do it?", and in the other instance, leading a child to ask, "What do they want me to do, and what do I get for doing it?" Neither strategy helps children to grapple with the question, "What kind of person do I want to be?"

REWARDS VS. ACHIEVEMENT

Rewards are no more helpful at enhancing achievement than they are at fostering good values. At least two-dozen studies have shown that people expecting to receive a reward for completing a task (or for doing it successfully) simply do not perform as well as those who expect nothing. This effect is robust for young children, older children, and adults; for males and females; for rewards of all kinds; and for tasks ranging from memorizing facts to designing collages to solving problems. In general, the more cognitive sophistication and open-ended thinking that is required for a task, the worse people tend to do when they have been led to perform that task for a reward.

There are several plausible explanations for this puzzling but remarkably consistent finding. The most compelling of these is that rewards cause people to lose interest in whatever they were rewarded for doing. This phenomenon, which has been demonstrated in a score of studies, makes sense given that "motivation" is not a single characteristic that an individual possesses to a greater or lesser degree. Rather, intrinsic motivation (an interest in the task for its own sake) is qualitatively different from extrinsic. Therefore, the questions educators need to ask is not how motivated their students are, but how their students are motivated. Start right, end right, and motivate, motivate, motivate!

In one representative study, young children were introduced to an unfamiliar beverage called ginger ale. Some were just asked to drink it; others were praised lavishly for doing so; a third group was promised treats if they drank enough. Those children who received either verbal or tangible rewards consumed more of the beverage than other children, as one might predict. But a week later these children found it significantly less appealing than they did before, whereas children who were offered no rewards liked it just as much as, if not more than, they had earlier. If we substitute reading or doing math or acting generously for drinking ginger ale, we begin to glimpse the destructive power of rewards. The data suggest that the more we want children to want to do something, the more counterproductive it will be to reward them for doing it.

D. L. Fountain describes the use of rewards as "power through seduction." Power, whether by intimidation or bribes, amounts to doing things to children rather than working with them. This ultimately frays associations, both among students and between students and adults.

Moreover, students who are encouraged to think about grades, stickers, or other "goodies" become less inclined to investigate ideas, think productively, and take chances. At least ten studies have shown that people presented a incentive generally choose the easiest feasible assignment. In the absence of rewards, by contrast, children are prone to pick tasks that are just outside of their current point of aptitude.

PRACTICAL IMPLICATIONS OF THE FAILURE OF REWARDS

The implications of this analysis and these data are troubling. If the question is "Do rewards motivate students?", the answer is, "Absolutely: they motivate students to get rewards." Unfortunately, that sort of motivation often comes at the expense of interest in, and excellence at, whatever they are doing. What is required, then, is nothing short of a transformation of our schools.

First, classroom management programs that rely on rewards and consequences ought to be avoided by any educator who wants students to take responsibility for their own behavior—and by any educator who places internalization of positive values ahead of mindless obedience. The alternative to bribes and threats is to work toward creating a caring community whose members solve problems collaboratively and decide together how they want their classroom environment to be.

Second, grades in particular have been found to have a detrimental effect on creative thinking, long-term retention, interest in learning, and preference for challenging tasks. These detrimental effects are not the result of too many bad grades, too many good grades, or the wrong formula for calculating grades. Rather, they result from the practice of grading itself, and the extrinsic orientation it promotes. Parental use of rewards or consequences to induce children to do well in school has a similarly negative effect on enjoyment of learning and, ultimately, on achievement. Avoiding these effects requires assessment practices geared toward helping students experience success and failure not as reward and punishment, but as information.

Finally, this distinction between reward and information might be applied to positive feedback as well. While it can be useful to hear about one's successes, and highly desirable to receive support and encouragement from adults, most praise is tantamount to verbal reward. Rather than helping children to develop their own criteria for successful learning or desirable behavior, praise can create a growing dependence on securing someone else's approval. Rather than offering unconditional support, praise makes a positive response conditional on doing what the adult demands. Rather than heightening interest in a task, the learning is devalued insofar as it comes to be seen as a prerequisite for receiving the teacher's approval.

CONCLUSION

In short, good ideals and ethics have to be grown from the inside out. Attempts to short-circuit this process by dangling rewards in front of children are at best ineffective, and at worst counterproductive. Children are likely to become enthusiastic, lifelong learners as a result of being provided with an engaging curriculum; a safe, caring community in which to discover and create; and a significant degree of choice about what they are learning. Rewards—like punishments—are unnecessary when these items are present. Try it out yourself and see "Whatever Works" in your classroom!

Chapter 6

ENCOURAGING AND EMPATHETIC LEARNING

During my past twenty years in the education field, I found my niche, as they say. My niche was teaching beginning teachers. I remember all of my wonderfully intuitive instructors at Duquesne University in Pittsburgh, Pennsylvania. I was truly a sponge drinking in everything that I could about elementary and special education. I wanted to model myself after them and help other "rookie" teachers see how special they were and how important their role was in our society.

Learning is about enhancing attentiveness, skills, and capabilities. It is an individual effect from a constant action of acquiring, retaining, and applying information to lend a hand in meeting unique individual needs. Significant questions for today's educators deal with providing character education, motivating students, mainstreaming special needs students, and integrating and minority students. The answer to these questions is "Encouraging and Empathetic Learning" strategies can provide a means to delivering a values-centered education, providing added stimulation and overcoming social detractors to academic excellence, and integrating and mainstreaming special-needs students as well as ethnic minority groups into the classroom without further segregating them.

The Encouraging and Empathetic Learning strategy is not a new teaching concept. It is an original thesis intended to assist under-prepared students. Since its start, it has evolved into several distinctive strategies and has verified functional for imparting non-cognitive skills as well as an awareness while providing freedom to students to achieve to their own potential. It also creates a sense of community within diverse backgrounds, recognizing the merit of all group members, not despite their differences in background, ability and experience, but because of them. The main tenants of "Encouraging and Empathetic Learning" are: emphasizing connection over detachment, fostering acceptance and support over measurement and assessment, and encouraging group partnership over individual competition. Group rewards are those anticipated returns based on the entire group's effort, however learning is calculated. Group rewards, and therefore group goals, produce many of the non-cognitive outcomes of cooperative learning. Task specialty refers to the techniques whereby each member is assigned an exact role or job sustaining the group assignment upon which the other group members depend.

Research shows that Encouraging and Empathetic Learning works! In forty-eight school programs studied, 78% of the E & E learning classes demonstrated considerably greater cognitive achievement over the control groups. This greater accomplishment is tied, however, to the presence of some form of individual accountability in evaluation. Research also shows that students help their group mates more in the E & E learning environment. Therefore, they gain doubly—in social status as well as academic achievement—because it is more in their interest to do so than in the traditional, competitive classroom.

Another complexity is that students do not automatically know how to arrange themselves in groups, let alone coordinate and prioritize their hard work. They find themselves in situations where they must converse, join forces, and prioritize, and are inexperienced in these skills. Also, research indicates that accomplishment and inspiration may lessen due to the effect of "diffused responsibility" experienced during group work. That is, one or two students tend to take charge and do all the work, or the group seeks the lowest acceptable effort. Other shortfalls include discrepancies among personalities within groups, individual desire, ability, teacher skills and preparation, and stage of implementation. However, since these shortfalls are generally common in and not overcome by traditional education and are prevalent in life in general, they actually solidify the reasons for adopting cooperative learning. If students, as adults, are supposed to face these problems throughout their lives, when better to introduce them to both problems and a relevant, collaborative, solution-oriented methodology than in the classroom and throughout their entire educational experience?

THE FOUNTAIN FOCUS: WHATEVER WORKS!

Having presented applicable information on E & E learning, I believe it portends solutions to four relevant problems facing educators and students today. Encouraging and Empathetic learning strategies offer appropriate methods to provide students with character education, motivation, a vehicle for mainstreaming, and better racial/ethnic integration. Since the biggest problems inhibiting the implementation of character education is reaching an agreement on which values should be taught and avoiding any perceived indoctrination method of teaching these values, E & E learning offers an attractive option.

This strategy allows them to take advantage of the opportunity to ask and investigate questions of personal interest and have a voice in deciding what they will learn. The teacher's role as facilitator and coach would side step the instruction charge as long as students' solutions are not predetermined or evaluated against a reestablished answer. The research possibilities and range of possible solutions make this attractive as students choose and discriminate among whatever sources they choose—parents, clergy and other. As students collaborate to reach and address possible solutions, they possibly achieve the ultimate goal of deriving a deeper understanding and conviction of values, far greater than memorizing and regurgitating a catechism of responses.

Encouraging and Empathetic Learning provides students the opportunity to reflect on complex issues, recast them in light of their own experiences and questions, to figure out for themselves—and one another—what kind of person one ought to be, which traditions are worth keeping, and how to proceed when two basic values seem to be in conflict. Thus, E & E learning serves not only as a loophole to a values-centered education, but a viable alternative for satisfactory instruction.

Chapter 7

TEACHING ACCOUNTABILITY

The word "order" and "discipline" brings many different meanings to our intellect. Control can be defined as "punishing students in order to make them perform." As in the Fountain FOCUS Discipline Approach, "Protocol" can also be defined as "teaching students to behave responsibly." Many of the "discipline" approaches used in other education programs spotlight on punishing students and using rewards to influence classroom behavior. However, given that discipline problems are often cited as the most challenging problem facing teachers today, I have looked at other approaches to address this pervasive problem

FOCUSing on discipline from the perspective of teaching students to behave responsibly can help us achieve many of our goals. Teaching students to assume accountability for their own behavior and learning is vital to the promotion of lasting participation in all relevant actions. Regarding others, valuing individual differences, and fair play are desirable outcomes of education. There are several models that have been successfully used as curricular frameworks to help teachers' structure their programs, adapt their teaching strategies, and involve their students in promoting personal and social responsibility.

The Fountain FOCUS Discipline Approach emphasizes attempts and self-direction as significant to the attainment of an individual's well-being. Respecting others' rights, considering others' feelings, and caring about others are critical to the accomplishment of collective well-being. D. L. Fountain places the achievement of these outcomes in an familiar sequence of levels or goals to help both teachers and students to become aware of their behaviors and to FOCUS their efforts as they move toward desired outcomes. Teachers can use these levels as a framework to prepare, teach, and assess student learning.

WHAT IS ACCOUNTABILITY?

The Fountain FOCUS Approach is described as moving from unreliability to accountability or dependability, moving from value for oneself and to revere and have concern for others. These behaviors would be first developed within the classroom environment and then used outside of the school, in the home and community settings.

Promoting understanding of the goals and different levels is integral to the success of the program. Teachers should take advantage of varied opportunities to help students learn about the program and the different levels. Teachers can use brief talks at the beginning of the class to discuss a level, use teachable moments during class to point out level-related activities, and invite students to share their experiences with different levels.

Experiencing different levels is important. Teachers can create opportunities by carefully selecting games that promote cooperation and inclusion and by offering experiences that help students see the relationship between effort and outcomes.

Selection is an integral part of each level. Students at Level I who misbehave or infringe on the rights of others can either choose to sit out or change their behaviors. Students also experience choices as they negotiate conflicts. At Level II, students can be allowed to choose their level of effort, providing their lack of effort does not adversely affect the performance of others. They could have the opportunity to select the number of repetitions of an exercise, choose from a series of progressively more difficult tasks at a station, or choose a level of game intensity—recreation or competitive. Choices at Level III may include choosing to work on activities related to personal goals or participating in teacher-directed activities. Level IV offers students the opportunity to choose to help other students in the class to learn.

Predicament Solving is incorporated into each level. At Level I students may address how to deal with name call or examine ways to negotiate a conflict. Level II problems may deal with issues of low motivation, while at Level II students may address difficulties they encounter in being self-directed. Dealing with peer pressure may be addressed at Level IV.

Expression encourages personal growth. Students can be asked to reflect on what they did and felt during class in relation to the levels. Reflection may also occur through writing, by a check list, in discussion, or even by a show of hands indicating how the students felt about an activity or behaviors during class.

Analysis time is need to talk to individuals about specific problems, teacher's observations in relation to levels, and how students view their behavior and class. This could be accomplished for some students during pre-class activities or games. Other students may require a greater length of time and may need to be seen outside of class.

The Fountain FOCUS Discipline Approach can be used to help teachers establish class rules and identify expectations for student behavior. Oftentimes teachers have too many and too constricted regulations. Many times rules are stated in stated in negative terms, emphasizing the don'ts rather than the do's. A few rules, coupled with clear expectations, can help children behave responsibly and reduce "discipline" problems.

SUMMARY

The Fountain FOCUS Discipline Approach offers teachers a magnificent structure for their instruction. The approach offers students procedures for their behavior, outlines expectations, and invites better involvement in knowledge. By empowering students, students learn self-control rather than being controlled through classroom management techniques. By changing our thinking about discipline, we can create positive learning environments that enriches the lives of students, both within the school and in the community.

To redress social pressures working against academic achievement, cooperative learning has been shown to increase student motivation since it satisfies many of the cognitive motivational needs. These include: maintaining interest, developing meaning or understanding, solving problems or making decisions, and linking current learning to existing knowledge. If applied to such subjective topics as values-centered education, it evens the playing field among superior, average, and below average achievers.

The key to motivation in the classroom is to maintain student interest in the material as well as interest in doing well. Research shows that in traditional classrooms, a zero sum game for grades, peer pressure works against achievement since achieving higher grades ultimately deprives another student of that grade. However in the E & E learning environment, peer pressure exerts the opposite effect since good grades also reflect well upon the group as a whole. Also, as students communicate and collaborate, their self-efficacy responds optimistically as they see a development toward achieving their objective and their direct involvement in the process.

I am some body.
The ME I see is the ME I'll be.
I can be courteous, conscientious, and creative.
I will SUCCEED.
I am a SUCCESS!

Chapter 8

ARE YOU SELF-DISCIPLINED?

"Self-control is the knack to get yourself to do something regardless the consequences of your poignant condition."
- D. L. Fountain

Envision what you could achieve if you could merely get yourself to follow all the way through on your finest intentions no matter what. Picture yourself saying to yourself, "You're failing and you want to pass the course." Without self-discipline that intention will never come to be in your lifetime. But with adequate self-discipline, it's a done pact. The peak of self-discipline is when you reach the point that when you make a conscious choice, and it's virtually certain that you will follow through on it.

Willpower is one of many personal growth tools available to you. Of course it is not a solution. Nevertheless, the problems which self-discipline can solve are important, and while there are other ways to solve these problems, self-discipline absolutely shreds them. Self-discipline can empower you to overcome any addiction or lose any amount of weight. It can wipe out procrastination, chaos, and lack of knowledge. Within the area of troubles it can solve, self-discipline is plainly unrivaled. Moreover, it becomes a powerful teammate when combined with other tools like enthusiasm, goal setting, and preparation.

BUILDING SELF-DISCIPLINE

The Fountain FOCUS Approach of how to build self-discipline is best explained by an parallel. Self-discipline is like strength. The more you use it, the stronger you become. The less you use it, the weaker you become.

Just as everyone has different levels of strength, we all possess different levels of self-discipline. Everyone has some—if you can hold your breath a few seconds, you have some self-discipline. But not everyone has developed his or her discipline to the same degree.

> *"Just as it takes muscle to build strength, it takes willpower to build self-discipline."*
> - D. L. Fountain

The way to build self-discipline is comparable to using strength training to build muscle. This means lifting weights that are close to your boundary. Note that when you strength train, you lift weights that are within your ability to lift. You push your muscles until they fail, and then you rest.

Similarly, the basic method to build self-discipline is to attempt challenges that you can successfully carry out but which are in close proximity to your limit. This doesn't mean trying something and failing at it every day, nor does it mean staying within your comfort zone. You will gain no strength trying to lift a weight that you cannot shift, nor will you gain strength lifting weights that are too light for you.

Strength training means that once you accomplish something, you increase the challenge. If you keep going on that way you won't get any stronger. Likewise, if you stop working to challenge yourself in life, you won't gain any more self-discipline.

Just as some individuals have average strength compared to how strong they could become with training, most people are very weak in their level of self-discipline.

It's a mistake to try to push yourself too hard when trying to build self-discipline. There's no shame in starting where you are. I recall when I first entered college in Pittsburgh; my first attempt at studying for 4 exams in one night was very weak. I was not as disciplined as I could have been.

Similarly, if you're very undisciplined right now, you can still use what little discipline you have to build more. The more disciplined you become, the easier life gets. Challenges that were once impossible for you will eventually seem like child's play. As you get stronger, the studying sessions will get easier, or the difficult job will become better, or the marriage therapy will seem to help out more and more, or the complicated goals will become your reality.

Don't compare yourself to other people. It won't help. You'll only find what you expect to find. If you think you're weak, everyone else will seem stronger. If you think you're strong, everyone else will seem weaker. There's no point in doing this. Simply look at where you are now, and aim to get better as you go forward.

Let's think about this circumstance:

Presume you want to develop the ability to study 3 hours each day, since you know it will make a real difference in your academic career. There is always plenty of room for improvement.

Perhaps you try to study 3 hours straight without succumbing to distractions, and you can only do it once. The next day you fail utterly. That's OK. You did study 3 hours for one day. Two is too much for you. So cut back a bit. What duration would allow you to study more than 2 days in a row (i.e. a whole week)? If you succeed (or if you feel that would be too easy), then increase the challenge for yourself.

Once you've mastered a week at one level, take it up a notch the next week. And continue with this studying manner until you've reached your goal.

While analogies like this are never perfect, I've gotten a lot of mileage out of this one. By raising the bar just a little each week, you stay within your capabilities and grow stronger over time. If you have any questions on the subject of classroom discipline (either specific or general) that you'd like to see addressed, feel free to post them as comments, and I do my best to post my answers.

Email me:

www.debrafountain.com

Chapter 9

PREVENTION STRATEGIES

Veteran teachers and administrators know only too well that concern for student misbehavior is not new—although the behavior problems have become more prevalent, violent, and destructive during the past 20 years. In study after study, conduct problems, lack of order, student protection, and hostility in the schools, make the top 10 list of concerns about public education. And these concerns are no longer directed only at middle and high schools. Very serious discipline problems are affecting elementary level schools as well.

As many elementary classroom teachers will tell you, they spend an inordinate amount of time and energy managing student misbehavior and conflict—time that could be spent on teaching and learning. A recent survey found that elementary students disrupt the classroom and talk back or rudely challenge the teachers repeatedly than they did a decade ago.

Lately, practitioners will wait until the behavior becomes serious enough to warrant referral(s) to special education or other intensive services. Sadly, the teachers and parents of too many of these students see signs of potential difficulty long before the behavior escalates to the point of referral—in some cases, by the end of first grade. Although many young children today partake in early childhood programs intended to thwart future learning problems, elementary school is a child's first understanding with recognized schooling. While many children easily adjust to the regulations and routines that define the code of conduct in public school classrooms, some students need more support in making this conversion.

"You need to address the problems in your classroom directly and immediately – preferably right at the beginning of the school year."
D. L. Fountain

Unfortunately, there has been little support for early intervention when a child shows signs of behavioral difficulties, and in some cases there have been significant barriers. For example, a clause in the 1997 reauthorization of the Individuals with Disabilities Education Act has inadvertently caused some administrators to refrain from discussing and addressing minor behavioral difficulties while others have begun automatically to refer students for the slightest infraction.

Administrators are wise to be concerned. The number of referrals continues to increase and the need to prevent many of these troublesome behaviors has never been so great. Fortunately, deterrence strategies do exist that enable school communities to readdress misconduct and reduce the potential for misbehavior early on, before the need for an official dialogue arises.

D. L. Fountain's discipline approach describes prevention practices that (PK-12) school administrators have found to be successful in accelerating school performance, increasing readiness for learning, and reducing problem behaviors. Creating a safe and organized school environment requires, among other things, having in place many precautionary measures for children's behavioral and emotional problems. This guide describes prevention practices that K-8 school administrators have found to be effective in accelerating school performance, increasing readiness for learning, and reducing problem behaviors. While these practices cannot prevent all inappropriate behaviors from occurring—indeed, administrators could implement all of the strategies in this guide and still experience behavioral problems for which they need more intensive strategies—they can help you create a school environment that promotes positive behavior.

This valuable information in my book derives from the work of researchers at six universities who spent the last six years implementing school-based prevention practices. Their FOCUS was on students with—and at risk of developing—emotional and behavioral disorders. Examples of prevention strategies from each of these projects are included throughout this document. Contact information for each project is found at the end of the document.

Research-based strategies varied across the districts represented in this guide, but one finding remained constant. First and foremost, administrators are key to making prevention work. Their role is twofold: providing an environment that fosters positive behavior and making available specialized support and services that can interrupt cycles of negative behavior.

FOCUS IDEA: Classroom and campus structural strategies. Practitioners provide continuous environments in classrooms and throughout the entire school. These approaches are designed to benefit all students by building uniform structure and a positive climate that promotes and supports appropriate behavior. Structural approaches, both those found within individual classrooms and those that are implemented school wide, typically address prevention from a multidimensional perspective that includes behavioral management, social skills instruction, and academic enrichment.

FOCUS IDEA: School as a pathway to family and community agency partnerships. Although classroom and school-wide structural strategies provide a stable and positive environment for most students, some students need additional support. Sound prevention strategies at this level establish linkages between the primary aspects of students' lives: home and family, school and classroom, and community and social service agencies. Family, school, and community agency partnerships can provide temporary assistance that can preempt the need for more intensive interventions.

Both types of prevention—working in tandem and on a consistent basis—are necessary.

Comprehensive school-based prevention strategies at the elementary level are relatively new. However, in most cases administrators will have some prevention strategies already in place. They can use these structures as building blocks as they work to establish a more comprehensive approach.

Prevention strategies can help administrators answer the following questions:

- What can be done in the classroom?
- What works school wide?
- How can we support students through school-family partnerships?
- How can we build community agency linkages?

Does your school have the following Fountain FOCUS practices?

Deterrence Practices in the Classroom
- Positive behavior management.
- Social skills instruction.
- Academic enrichment.

School-wide Deterrence Program
- Unified discipline approach.
- Shared expectations for social competent behavior.
- Academic enrichment.

School-Family-Community Prospectus
- Parent partnerships.
- Community Services.

DETERRENCE PRACTICES IN THE CLASSROOMS

Administrators know that effective classroom practices—such as good classroom organization, engaging lessons with high rates of student response, positive climates, accommodations to match students' ability levels, and mild consequences for misbehavior—usually will lead to appropriate behaviors for the majority of students. However, many of today's students often require additional support.

Prevention approaches in classrooms FOCUS on what students need to be successful. They extend the practitioner's reach in helping students before corrective measures are necessary. Prevention has two important advantages over corrective, after-the-fact discipline. First, it tends to be cost effective—it is much easier to prevent inappropriate behaviors than it is to correct them. Second, there are no negative consequences for children who behave appropriately.

In most classroom and schoolwide prevention approaches, there is an emphasis on:

- Behavior management systems that teach and reward appropriate behaviors.
- Social skills instruction as an integral part of the curriculum.
- Academic enrichment to ensure that students master key knowledge and skills.

POSITIVE BEHAVIOR MANAGEMENT

Prevention through classroom management typically FOCUSes on developing appropriate student behaviors, accelerating classroom learning, and decreasing inappropriate behaviors. Features of positive classroom management include:

- Clearly communicated expectations for student behavior. Teachers define acceptable behaviors in a concrete manner. Acceptable and desired behaviors are within reach for the students.

- Ongoing positive and corrective feedback. Teachers tell students what they are doing correctly and praise them for appropriate behavior. In addition, teachers redirect inappropriate behavior before more intensive interventions become necessary.

- Fair and consistent treatment of students. Rules, consequences, and enforcement procedures are clearly defined and articulated to all students. There are no surprises; students know what is expected and what will happen if they deviate from the established system. The posted rules and mild consequences are fair and applied consistently to all students.

An important element of positive behavior management is teaching students to monitor their own behaviors. Self-monitoring provides students with a strategy for observing their own behavior, recording it, and evaluating how they did. Typically, self-monitoring strategies consist of teacher cues, a student checklist of appropriate behaviors, and systematic reinforcement for progress. Self-monitoring helps students internalize their behavior and provides a visual reminder of what is expected of them.

CLASSROOM PREVENTION IN ACTION: POSITIVE BEHAVIOR MANAGEMENT

An increase in academic engagement, in seat behavior, and in positive student interaction—what administrator would not want a strategy that delivered these results? The Behavior Prevention Program works with educators to develop classroom management systems that FOCUS on helping students develop these and other positive behaviors.

In the Behavior Prevention Program approach, teachers identify their expectations and teach the appropriate behaviors directly. Key instructional strategies include modeling, providing practice, rewarding good behavior, and having students self-monitor their progress. Teachers find that this approach increases their use of praise and reinforcement of proactive skills—a powerful strategy in teaching students how to behave.

The Good Student Game is an example of how teachers can FOCUS on promoting positive behaviors using a class monitoring system. Teachers teach and monitor positive behaviors (e.g., staying seated and working quietly) and students learn how to self-monitor these behaviors.

The steps to the Good Student Game are:

- Identify when to play the game.
- Identify and clearly define behaviors to be rewarded.

- Set goals for individual and group performance.
- Select rewards (e.g., pencils, notebooks, extra time at recess, etc.).
- Set the monitoring interval (e.g., variable or intermittent intervals when students will assess and record their own behavior).
- Teach the game procedures to students.
- Play the game.

Consider the following example. Mr. Perry, a fourth grade teacher, taught a diverse group of youngsters. In addition to typical students, there were students with attention problems, students with learning and behavioral difficulties, limited-English-proficiency students, and gifted students. Classroom management was a constant struggle.

Students had trouble following directions and completing assignments. Since many students had particular difficulty during independent work times, Mr. Perry decided to use the Good Student Game during those periods to keep students on-task. To support this goal, he identified the following behaviors:

- Stay seated.
- Raise your hand if you have a question.
- Work quietly.
- Raise your hand when you finish.

Next, Mr. Perry set performance goals and rewards. In order to receive 10 minutes of free time at the end of the day, all students were expected to demonstrate the appropriate behaviors 80% of the time. Because students routinely asked (and sometimes pleaded) for free time, Mr. Perry felt confident that students would value this reward.

Mr. Perry taught the Good Behavior Game procedures to students in a 20-minute session. To set the context, he began by having students discuss the relationship between good behavior and classroom success. He then presented the behaviors, modeled them, and gave students ample opportunities to practice them.

Finally, he showed students how their behavior would be monitored. By participating in the Good Behavior Game, students learned to self-monitor their behavior. Over time, students internalized the appropriate behaviors.

SOCIAL SKILLS INSTRUCTION

Teachers must be clear about their expectations regarding social skills. We may say we expect students to listen, to show respect, to cooperate, to be responsible, and to resolve conflicts. However, unless we make sure students understand what we mean and what they are supposed to do, we cannot expect compliance.

Social skills instruction includes classroom survival skills (e.g., listening, answering questions, asking for help) and critical peer skills (e.g., cooperating, showing empathy, making friends). Most elementary aged students can benefit from social skills instruction. But students with behavior problems often have social skill deficits that put them at a distinct disadvantage in classroom and schoolwide interactions.

Effective social skills instruction also can affect classroom management practices. For example, many classroom routines require that students demonstrate good social skills (e.g., listen, ask politely, cooperate, share materials). Teaching social skills can help to clarify teacher expectations and help students understand how they should behave.

Social skills instruction also can help improve social interactions and reduce problem behavior. An increasingly common view holds that some students who misbehave do so because they lack the social skills necessary for making more appropriate choices. In this context, social skills become "replacement behaviors"—we teach students how to behave appropriately so they will make the "right" choices. For instance, a child may respond in anger by hitting another child because he or she has not been taught acceptable alternatives.

Examples of social skills programs that support prevention include:

- Skillstreaming the Elementary School Child
- Teaching Social Skills: A Practical Instructional Approach
- Skills for Living

CLASSROOM PREVENTION IN ACTION: SOCIAL SKILLS INSTRUCTION

Today's students bring to the classroom a diversity of background experiences and social learnings. Too often, students fail at tasks because they have not developed the social skills they need to succeed.

Project SUCCESS recommends teaching social skills as part of the curriculum. The components of the Project SUCCESS approach are:

- Define the social skill to be taught in observable terms.
- Teach the social behaviors that make up the skill.
- Model the skill.
- Engage students in practicing the skill.
- Provide reinforcement and feedback for skill performance.
- Have students self-monitor their behaviors.

Although some teachers choose to teach social skills as a subject area in its own right, others integrate social skills instruction throughout the curriculum. Project SUCCESS links social skills instruction with activity or lesson requirements because most instructional formats—discussion, cooperative learning, peer tutoring, group problem solving, etc.—require social as well as academic skills. If students do not have the social prerequisites for participating in an activity (e.g., listening, following directions, asking questions, etc.), they may respond with off-task and other inappropriate behaviors.

Using the Project SUCCESS model, teachers teach the social skills that support participation in academic activities. For example, students may be expected to solve a math story problem in groups, discuss the characters in a story during literacy circle, or use a writing process to edit a partner's writing. Teachers teach the social skills concurrently with the academic content.

Project SUCCESS also recommends teaching social skills that are linked to classroom rules. Consider this example. Ms. T posted the following classroom rules:

- Listen to my teacher and follow her directions.
- Stay in my seat unless I have permission to leave.
- Stop talking when my teacher tells me.

Although Ms. T phrased the rules clearly and in a positive manner, she questioned whether the students had the necessary social skills to comply. For example, she had to ask the class repeatedly to listen while she was talking. At one point she became so frustrated with several students that she exclaimed, "Why don't you ever listen?" She was very surprised to find later that even though these youngsters had been chatting, they had been following her directions for completing their assignment.

Ms. T decided that some of her students probably did not know how to listen. As she thought more about her dilemma, she questioned whether or not she had made her expectations for social behavior clear to the students. To enhance their social skills, Ms. Trujillo decided to teach listening skills—specifically the subskill, "letting the listener know you are listening"—using the Project SUCCESS approach. As part of instruction, she had students self-monitor their progress in every lesson and class activity.

ACADEMIC ENRICHMENT

Students with learning difficulties sometimes exhibit behavioral problems. For example, the student who has difficulty staying on task during reading group may have an underlying reading problem that should be assessed Academic tutoring—and especially peer tutoring—is often cited as a viable prevention strategy. Peer tutoring can have a positive effect on student learning, is cost effective, and can be effective in improving both the tutor's and tutee's social.

SCHOOL-WIDE DETERRENCE PROGRAM

Teachers can use universal prevention strategies in their classrooms to achieve positive student outcomes. Results may be even better, however, when the entire school staff is committed to universal prevention and when there is a school-wide learning environment that promotes positive academic, behavioral, and social-emotional outcomes for all students.

Positive behavior management, social skills instruction, and academic enrichment techniques form the basis for a school-wide approach. Throughout the school day and across all school environments students should be encouraged to adapt their behavior to the school setting. Expectations for behavior, rules, and consequences should be consistent. School-wide prevention approaches support adaptive behavior; school-wide structures enable all staff to identify signs of problems early and to take steps to resolve them.

- Unified discipline approach. Throughout the school there are clearly defined expectations and rules for appropriate behavior, with common consequences and clearly stated procedures for correcting problem behaviors.

- Shared expectations for socially competent behavior. School-wide support plans address social and behavioral needs by helping students learn to manage their own behavior. The emphasis is on teaching students how to solve conflicts, be responsible, and behave in socially appropriate ways as members of a learning community.

When schools implement a unified discipline plan, they can expect the following outcomes:

- Improved student behavior, including time on task.
- Decreased discipline issues and office referrals.
- Improved staff and student attitudes.

Here is an example while I was working for the Broward County School Board:

As part of the Park Ridge School Improvement Plan, Principal Dudley and his faculty identified high rates of office referrals, inconsistent approaches to classroom management, and low teacher morale related to discipline. Mr. Dudley decided that a school-wide discipline approach was needed and knew that he needed to set the tone for the school.

First, Mr. Dudley presented the cohesive discipline approach to his staff and encouraged them to adopt it. He was a first year principal with brand new teachers. He would also have to speak with the few veteran teachers in the school too. He was truly a confident, positive, and buoyant individual who was a fantastic leader of our school.

After securing unanimous support for the approach, he engaged all personnel in identifying expectations and consequences to be implemented across all grade levels. This afforded staff opportunities to discuss concerns and arrive at consensus regarding expectations for appropriate behavior and how transgressions should be handled. From this point, a small group set about writing the plan, which was later circulated for review and discussion.

Once the plan was in final form, staff explained it to the students. A monitoring system was put into place to track office referrals and classroom discipline issues. After the first year of implementation, the results were impressive. Office referrals showed a significant decrease, as did classroom rule violations.

> *"We used a combination peer mediation and conflict resolution program for three years in urban Broward County schools, Florida, with students from varied socioeconomic and racial backgrounds. I found it very useful in allowing students to develop the skills needed to solve their own problems without adult help. In a middle school where I taught 7th grade (Chapter I, self-contained, and at-risk) students, a program was set up for "Peer Promise and Resolution" who were more willing to take care of conflicts when they shared their troubles with other students rather than adults."*
> – D. L. Fountain

Handling conflicts is a significant challenge for early adolescents. Students of all ages typically rely on withdrawal or use of aggression. They can benefit from training in how to handle conflicts in socially appropriate ways.

Stemming conflict through peer mediation and conflict resolution is the goal of the Conflict Resolution/Peer Intervention Mission. To reduce the incidence of peer conflict, all students receive social skills training in conflict resolution, with selected students learning mediation skills. These "peer mediators" have the opportunity to demonstrate positive social skills for resolving disputes on a regular basis.

The results can be impressive. After training in conflict resolution and peer mediation:

- ♦ Students tend to resolve conflicts through discussion and negotiation procedures.
- ♦ Students' attitudes toward conflict and the school climate tend to be more positive.
- ♦ Students' psychological health and self-esteem tend to improve.
- ♦ Discipline problems and suspensions tend to decrease.

The Conflict Resolution/Peer Intervention Mission helps students develop interpersonal skills that lead to positive social behavior and constructive conflict management. The project approach consists of the following components:

♦ A school-wide conflict resolution curriculum. The purpose of the curriculum is to provide a constructive approach to conflict and to provide students with skills that can help them find productive resolutions. Social skills for conflict resolution include: understanding conflict, communicating effectively, understanding and handling anger, and mediating peer disagreements.

- A peer mediation program. Each school selects a group of 20-35 students who receive special training in mediation skills. Social mediation skills include: understanding conflict, maintaining confidentiality, communicating effectively, and listening. The students who complete the training successfully serve as school-wide peer mediators for the year.

- School-wide structure for conflict mediation. When students cannot resolve their own conflicts, they may refer themselves or be referred to peer mediation sessions. Peer mediation sessions are scheduled as part of the formal school schedule. Referrals to peer mediation can be made by students, teachers, or administrative staff. Pairs of mediators use structured mediation procedures to help disputants come to mutually satisfactory agreements.

Let's follow the peer mediation process where I worked in a northeastern middle school located in Levittown, New York. To formalize the referral process, school staff members developed a referral protocol and schedule for mediations. Staff members knew that it was important to accommodate disputants in a timely manner with minimal disruption of academic activities, so they set aside homeroom period for peer mediation sessions. Homeroom offered an environment in which routine supervision could be kept to a minimum, but also ensured that a teacher or counselor would be available if needed.

To initiate the protocol for a mediation, students or staff used a referral form that included the following information:

- Referring party.
- Conflict location.
- Brief description of the problem.
- Names of the disputants.

Once a referral was made, a mediation was scheduled. Two peer mediators met with the students to help them resolve their conflict constructively and to prevent the problem from escalating. At the end of each mediation, the peer mediators completed a peer mediation agreement form that was signed by the mediators and the disputants. This type of mediation worked for my schools – maybe it can work for you, your school, and district!!

Chapter 10

WHAT DO I DO NOW?

ARTICLE FOR ACP 2005 CANDIDATES (DISTRIBUTED AT MOTIVATION WORKSHOP)

There is a remarkable amount of investigation today on motivation in the classroom. Across the country, classroom teachers are constantly asking the question of motivation. Research indicates that even though motivation may be inherent in the student, the classroom is where it takes place. Teachers, parents, and administrators are faced with the task of enriching, enlightening, and increasing the desire to learn in students each and every day. Motivation seems to be decreasing in classrooms and much research is being done to find out why and what can be done.

A motivating discussion about motivation poses this problem. If a student does poorly in class and also has low motivation, does the student do poorly because of low motivation or is low motivation causing the student to do poorly. This is a thought provoking debate. Each and every student has individual needs and personal factors that effect motivation. To understand the range of the issue of motivation, one must recognize the components of motivation, the factors that influence motivation or a lack of motivation, and what researchers say can be done to increase motivation in the classroom.

Motivation is essentially an internal condition, whether it is inborn or whether it is acquired. The desire to learn itself is natural. We come into this world willing to gain understanding about out surroundings. Motivated students have a desire to be involved in the learning process, which is usually accompanied by a reason or a goal for being involved Many students may be equally motivated to perform but have different goals or reasons for performing. This is where intrinsic and extrinsic motivation comes into play.

Students can be intrinsically motivated to perform because they enjoy the activity or they simply like the feeling they get from doing it, while others may be extrinsically motivated because they want to obtain the reward or avoid the punishment. Students do have different reasons for motivation. Intrinsic motivation is the desire to engage in an activity for its own sake and extrinsic motivation is a desire for the reward that follows the engagement. There have been several studies that found positive correlations between intrinsic motivation and academic achievement. "Most of the work has been correlation and therefore cannot assume that motivation causes achievement to go up or down. At least one researcher has concluded there is a causal relationship: reduced intrinsic motivation produces achievement deficits."

A number of other studies have shown that extrinsic motivators such as stickers, extra points, etc. reduce creativity and result in a poorer job done by the student. However, if teachers remove these rewards from the classroom, many students will quit working. Some students are only motivated by these rewards. The effectiveness of rewards is questionable. One study revealed that extrinsic rewards were no more effective in increasing motivation in typically unmotivated students than simple requests to work on the tasks. Students who are intrinsically motivated prefer tasks that are more challenging, while extrinsically motivated students gravitate toward tasks with a low degree of difficulty. They put minimal effort into maximum reward.

There are many factors that influence the development of student motivation. According to D. L. Fountain, "motivation to study and learn is a competence acquired through general experience but stimulated most frankly through modeling, communication of expectations, and direct instruction and socialization by parents and teachers." As D. L. Fountain puts it, "seldom does one hear a parent criticize that their student in pre-kindergarten is unmotivated."

THE FOUNTAIN FOCUS:
WHATEVER WORKS!

Parents are the first teachers in a child's life. Children come into the world with a yearning to learn and a powerful need to make sense of their environment. Parents pass on to their children a certain attitude about learning and it can be positive or negative. This attitude influences how children view the process of learning and can change as children progress through school. "Their perceptions of their ability actually decrease and they tend to reflect the teacher's evaluation of their ability." This is one reason why the teacher's role is so valuable in the motivation process. It is actually the responsibility of the classroom teacher to motivate. According to D. L. Fountain," every child is motivated, it is the teachers job to get them motivated to what they want them to do." She also states that in order to be motivated, three things need to be present:

FOCUS #1—The objective must be attractive.

FOCUS #2—The amount of effort it would take to accomplish the objective is practical.

FOCUS #3—They must consider the likeliness of achievement that they will attain the goal.

The principles of motivation apply to all of us, in spite of age. We learn when we have a reason for learning. Students need to see the association between what they are learning in the classroom and their own individual goals. How will this lesson relate to the future? They also must have a definite amount of success. Children with low motivation need a positive approach to learning as they search for motivation. The subject matter must somehow be more attractive and the student must acquire a sense of being able to attain the goals. With continued success and support, an unmotivated student can become motivated. Another factor that can influence motivation is personal priority. Some children may rank information as low on their scale of priority. Motivation can function independently of the lure of the subject matter. In this case, a student may have a good reason to lose interest or motivation.

A first FOCUS step in helping motivate students in the classroom is for teachers to recognize that each student's goal is to be successful while protecting their self-worth. They need to feel confident in their ability to succeed. "Students' self-worth is tied to their self-concept of ability in school settings. This self-concept of ability has significant consequences for student achievement. In the classroom, all tasks can be made important through the use of external rewards and certain evaluation procedures."

In order for students to participate fully in the process of learning, they must experience the classroom as a caring, supportive place where they are valued and respected. A variation of tasks in the classroom can enhance motivation. Tasks need to be challenging but achievable.

Relevance is a terrific promoter of motivation!! If the teacher can convince the student that what they are working for is significant, then they will be more motivated to complete the assignment. What takes place in the classroom is vital, but "the classroom is not an island." To support motivation, classroom teachers should FOCUS on learning, task mastery, and effort, instead of how well students execute and participate.

The complex array of problems that contribute to low levels of motivation makes it difficult to come up with an approach that will make unmotivated students want to learn. Student motivation is an ongoing process that requires much creativity and energy on the part of every classroom teacher. Teachers must learn to show students that success is important for them now and in their future.

If teachers have a better understanding of the components of motivation, the factors that influence motivation or lack of motivation and some things that can be done to help motivate students in their classroom, then they will be successful in helping students acquire the motivation needed to gain new knowledge. You CAN build the Fountain FOCUS classroom atmosphere where your students feel successful and are excited to learn!
Questions or comments regarding this topic:

www.debrafountain.com

Chapter11

INVOLVE YOUR STUDENTS

It all seems uncomplicated. The instructor plans a great lesson. Everyone comes to class. The instructor presents the material. The students learn it. Everyone is happy and goes home! Why doesn't it always end this way?

We know what a functional, well-managed classroom looks like. Above all, it is instructor controlled. The instructor is in charge, but the learning is student driven and student centered. This ideal classroom isn't necessarily quiet in fact it probably isn't but the noise emanating from this classroom is clearly related to on-task behavior. Students discuss the lesson among themselves and with the instructor. The sounds of "practical application" can be heard from bell to bell. It is what every career-technical instructor longs for but doesn't always get.

Why do so many classrooms consist of students talking back to teachers, fighting with each other, and sitting around doing much of nothing? The problem is clear, even if the solution is not.

So, what can teachers do to invalidate this trend? What are the secrets to effective classroom management? Unfortunately, there are no secrets to effective classroom management, but if there were, the following would certainly be included.

FOCUS TIP 1—**Have understandable and direct expectations for your students:**

Students often misbehave because they are unsure of what is expected of them. Rules, policies and procedures should be clearly stated and taught to the students during the first or second day of class. This lesson on rules should include major, as well as minor, safety rules and should include overall rules of personal conduct. Annoying behaviors that are personally offensive to the instructor or other members of the class should especially be discussed. Often, relatively minor offensives become major distractions that could easily have been avoided. Theorists over the past few decades have suggested that teachers should have only three to five rules, including vague statements such as, "Be nice to each other," and, "Obey the teacher." This theory has good intention, but it leaves many unspecified actions not addressed and capable of causing havoc in a classroom or lab. It is much more likely that students will behave appropriately if they know exactly what the standards for behavior are.

As a teacher gains experience in a specific course and lab, he/she will know which infractions are most disruptive and most likely to occur. Rules preventing their occurrence and consequences associated with their occurrence should be emphasized. Once in the workforce, young workers will be exposed to a myriad of safety and other workplace rules and regulations.

FOCUS TIP 2—**Deal with a problem without delay!**

Even with clear expectations, infractions of the rules of proper behavior are predictable. Teachers should consider means of correcting the behavior that can be administered during the class period in which the infraction occurs. We've all heard the stories of children who are warned by a parent, "Wait until your father/mother comes home!" This is fine if Dad/Mom is coming home soon, but if he or she is off on business for a week, any reprimand that is inflicted will probably not be effectively associated with the offensive behavior. In addition, everyone involved will likely be miserable waiting for the "big day," and otherwise valuable and meaningful experiences will be lost waiting for the consequences to play out. Likewise, carrying problems in the classroom from one day to the next interferes with multiple days of instruction. Using techniques such as verbal warnings, redirection of student behavior and other immediate consequences can lessen lost instructional time due to urgent corrections and behavior modifications.

FOCUS TIP 3—**Treat all students with r-e-s-p-e-c-t!**

A key element in assuming leadership of a classroom is to convey to students that they are important and that the teacher is confident that they can master the content. Teachers should commit themselves to learning each student's name during the first two or three days. Calling students by their names makes them feel part of the classroom organization. Teachers should smile and show enthusiasm; no one will be interested in a subject that clearly bores the instructor.

Teachers should model appropriate behaviors such as patience, a sense of humor, courtesy and manners. Some students are not exposed to appropriate interpersonal courtesies in the home and may not even be accustomed to asking permission to use another person's pencil, saying "excuse me" after a cough or sneeze, or saying "thank you" and "please."

In order to teach respect, teachers must be committed to modeling respect. Even during a reprimand, teachers should preserve the dignity of the student. When the reprimand is over, teachers should not hold a grudge and punish the student further by ignoring him/her for days afterwards or by making nonverbal gestures. This causes problems to grow and causes learning not to take place.

After a teacher decides the objective and the level of assessment, he/she should use teaching methodologies that include a stimulating introduction to the lesson and step-by step instructions on how to perform a particular task or complete a particular project. Middle school and high school students need to hear rules and concepts more than once. New teachers often feel that they are repeating themselves unnecessarily, but in reality, the first time some students hear something is the second or third time the teacher says it. During the lecture or demonstration, he/she should integrate visual, auditory and concrete teaching aids.

There should be several periods of question-and-answer sessions for the teacher to determine whether or not students understand. This question-and-answer session also provides an occasion for the teacher to call on students by name and for them to be given vocal praise for accurate responses.

Students should then be given time for independent practice. The teacher should move around the room inspecting the advancement of each student. It is during this time period that teachers can monitor whether their instruction was successful. This also provides a time for the teacher to regroup and clarify a particular step and give individual support if necessary.

FOCUS TIP 4—**Fill each period with activity.**

When do most students get into trouble? Chances are it is when they don't have much to do. Most problems occur at the beginning of class or at the end of class when students are not on task. This can also be a problem in classrooms where the students are allowed to remain off task during instructional time. The key to eliminating this undesired behavior is to fill each period with significant activity from "bell to bell."

Consistently use an introduction activity at the beginning of the class, such as vocabulary activities, tools of the day, brainteasers, etc., while administrative tasks are being performed. Plan instruction that lasts until a minute or two before the students will leave the classroom or laboratory. Have a plan for unanticipated class delays, such as visitors or other interruptions. In short, keep the students too busy to get into trouble!

FOCUS TIP 5—**Monitor your students.**

When possible, don't let them get out of your sight. Eliminate or redirect administrative duties that are performed during class time that take you away from watching your students. Eliminate unsupervised areas of your classroom and lab. Avoid sending students into unsupervised work areas, unless it is necessary, safe and meets the policy of your organization. Wear comfortable shoes, and move among the students. Make each student a "front-row student."

FOCUS TIP 6—**Deal with problems at the lowest possible level.**

It's true. Principals do not generally think very highly of teachers who can't handle their own discipline problems and constantly refer students to them for discipline. Coincidentally, neither do students. Teachers should develop a discipline plan with consequences that can be administered within the classroom. Make referrals to a higher authority an extreme measure that will carry a substantial amount of weight, because it happens so infrequently. For the most part, students respect instructors who are confident, fair, firm and consistent. When outside intervention is required, follow school policy. Chances are this policy begins in the classroom, expands to include parents and then involves administrators if earlier intervention fails. Of course, there are exceptions for violent behavior or the breaking of laws, such as the possession of drugs or weapons, so be familiar with school policy. But, for the most part, teachers should not give up their authority or influence until they are confident that they have done all that can be done.

FOCUS TIP 7—**Pick your battles carefully.**

Some battles are not worth fighting. Some behaviors are worse than others. Teachers should carefully consider whether a behavior is worth the trouble of correction. This is not to mean that inappropriate behavior should be ignored, but instead that the inappropriateness of the behavior should be considered. Should students be sitting in their desks when the bell rings or is it acceptable for them to simply be inside the classroom when the bell rings? Should they be silent while working in the lab or can they talk quietly? When the bell rings to end class, are the students allowed to get up and leave or do they have to be dismissed verbally by the instructor? These may be considered minor issues or major issues, depending on the preferences of the teacher. In any case, they can be the beginning of a battle that becomes a major battle. Teachers have to come to a decision if the behavior is worth the battle.

FOCUS TIP 8—**Think like a kid, but act like an adult.**

It's often said that teaching can keep a person young. This "youthfulness" can be a great asset to a teacher in the classroom. Teachers should take time to understand what it is like to be a youth in the community, pay attention to the music and movies that students like, and try to appreciate their clothing styles and food preferences. Then, this understanding can be used to design activities that will appeal to students. Teachers should try to relate instructional activities to things that are important to their students.

At the same time, young students need guidance from adults. They need role models and good examples to help shape their attitudes and actions. Adults and teachers don?t need to try to dress like them, and they don't have to like their music, but they do need to demonstrate concern and responsibility that students can feel and see. Teachers must keep their "cool," even when students lose theirs.

FOCUS TIP 9—**Keep the lines clear between the instructor and the student.**

New teachers have to be especially sensitive to the well-drawn line between students and themselves. Younger teachers find it easier to be role models to middle and high school students, because their ages and interests are more similar. However, it is sometimes more difficult for younger teachers to keep clear lines between the two relationships. Verbal and nonverbal cues are the best way to maintain a healthy relationship. Statements such as, "I want you to feel free to talk to me about things that are going on in your life," will welcome students to share life experiences with a teacher. Teachers should encourage this. But, the sharing should not be as open the other way. Teachers, especially young teachers, need to be careful to keep their personal lives personal. Doing otherwise confuses high school students and makes them feel that the teacher is just another friend, companion or confidant. This close relationship can be dangerous and cause employment and sexual harassment issues.

On the other hand, students do need good role models. Since teachers interact with these young people daily, are well educated and are usually of good moral standards, they are ideal counselors and coaches. This opportunity to influence the lives of young people is awesome, and if handled correctly, can be one of the most rewarding experiences presented to us as human beings.

FOCUS TIP 10—**Care about the students!**

Some people seem to have an instinctive ability to nurture students. Other people have to make conscious efforts to exhibit concern. Either way, teachers should communicate to students that they want them to be successful in and out of the classroom. Teachers should attend sporting events, club functions, plays, programs and other activities in which their students are involved. These provide opportunities for teachers to see their students in a different setting and recognize other talents a student may have. These events also provide a chance for teachers to network with parents in an unbiased setting. Complimenting students on their accomplishments and talents builds esteem.

Another imperative tool is the telephone. When a student is absent for more than a couple of days, the teacher should make a quick phone call during his/her planning period or after school to let the student know that he/she is missed and to find out if the illness or situation is serious.

Teachers should always acknowledge students in the hallways at school and away from school. Long conversations usually have to be avoided because of time constraints, but a simple smile and a hello is valuable in building a caring relationship. Teachers should be aware of who their students are associated with. These associations can help explain a change in behavior or performance in the classroom.

Considering the many elements discussed in this article, teachers will agree that there is no one secret to classroom management. There are, however, several key elements in being a successful classroom manager. Teachers should be committed to staying abreast of new techniques for classroom management, just as they should stay up to date on current trends affecting young people. It is very easy to become complacent and outdated. But, the rewards are greater for teachers who commit to being involved with their students and take the time to make a difference in their students' lives. Many conscientious teachers regard their students as extended family, and some stay in touch with each other for a lifetime! I have kept with many of former students from a number of states where I have worked…my own 3 children love to hear from all of them!!

Chapter12

CONSEQUENCES FOR NEGATIVE BEHAVIOR

When we look at all the research and studies, we see that both parents and the public expect elementary schools to provide a high-quality education for their children. We know that this is not possible without safe and orderly classrooms where students can concentrate on learning without the threat of constant disruptions or incidents of violence. It seems that everyday in the U.S. we see more and more reports in the news involving discipline problems especially in inner-city schools. Although the elementary school system is not perfect when it comes to discipline, we as educators should direct ourselves to take back control of our classrooms at all grade levels.

When we think about discipline in our elementary schools most of the public does not see a problem. But yet for a majority of our nations inner-city elementary schools discipline is a real problem. Discipline is not just a problem for educators; it is also a problem for other students wanting to learn.

Along with the serious acts of discipline, there were also the disruptive students. These are the students that disrupt classrooms and school activities. These students are the ones that usually cause trouble by doing such things as teasing other students, and being bullies. In my 20+ years of conducting my own research, I found that this involved " harassment in the form of verbal threats, bullying, and name calling" There are also those students that are disruptive in school by spreading rumors, interpersonal arguments, and misunderstandings.

When we look at some of the reasons why inner-city elementary schools experience a discipline problem. We see that this is only a part of an overall problem that is destroying many of our nation's urban communities. Over the last 20+ years, I saw many problems including: unemployment, crime, child abuse, neglect, and addiction to drugs and alcohol. These are major contributors to the growing problem of discipline in inner-city education.

Discipline in inner-city elementary schools apparently has no one real factor controlling it. The reasons may be many but they all seem to concentrate on one thing, money. In our urban neighborhoods one can clearly see that usually many of the buildings in the area are run down, and this along with school districts that are not willing to invest in improving our inner-city schools, this can have a clear influence on the attitudes of our nations children and in the end may be the one factor that really counts.

After looking at all the problems that teachers are forced to deal with in inner-city schools, one can see that the only real solution is to deal with the problem. I taught in inner-city elementary and middle schools in 5 different states. We, as educators, must take a cold hard look at what is really causing discipline problems and we must make every effort to correct it:

- Never use something you want a child to care for as a consequence.

- When you take something away (a pattern), give something back (a new performance).

- Eventually you must face a student that misbehaves. No one can do it for you.

- When disciplining students, always provide both choices and limits.

- No one can change her or his pattern without being dedicated and determined.

- When they do something well, use praise, praise, and more praise!

There is no one magic bullet that will put an end to disciplinary problems. There is also no one philosophy that will work every time, but I believe that by using a "Whatever Works" philosophy like the Fountain FOCUS Approach along with the proper attitude on the educators part, and a school system that is open to new ideas and methods. Then, our school systems might be able to resolve the problem of discipline.

Chapter 13

STRUCTURE BEFORE INSTRUCTION

During my teaching preparation at Duquesne University, I used to think that the scariest thing about teaching was staying in control of a whole classroom full of kids. I figured that if I would be very commanding, and they would all listen to me. You may have heard the old saying, "Don't smile until Thanksgiving." Baloney! Smile the first day! Smile every day! Don't try to intimidate them. It won't work. Thirty kids can take one teacher any day of the week if they really want to!

But, you ask, what do I do to keep order in the classroom? Surprisingly enough, the children really want to learn and they want school to be a place where there is order. They want you to be in charge. But they want you to be friendly and approachable.

Respecting the children as human beings is the most important aspect of keeping control of your class. It took me a long time to realize this. Remember that you are teaching real people with feelings. Think how you would feel if someone spoke to you the way you've heard many teachers speak to their students. Make it clear that you intend to respect them and expect them to return the favor.

Don't mistake popularity for respect. Popularity is like a shiny penny, attractive, but not valuable. Respect is valuable. The children don't need you to be their buddy. They have a class full of buddies. They need someone to be the adult, but an adult who respects them.

G. G. R.—Give and Get Respect

The next time you speak to your class, speak to them the way you would speak to your friends or acquaintances.

During my second year of teaching:
I turned in my lesson plans to my principal and they were not done to her specifications. She walked into the teacher's lounge and loudly reprimanded me in front of my colleagues. She even labeled me as a little careless. How would you feel? When she left the room what would say – or want to say to your friends?

After that year, I decided to pursue my master's degree in educational leadership and become a principal. I knew that this principal did not like a lot of the new teachers. She did not have the patience with her faculty or the students in the school. I knew that I could do it BETTER…and I DID!

When I became the principal of my own school years later, I had to deal with a new teacher that I hired. I asked Bryan to come to my office and showed him where he needed to improve his lesson plans. I listened to his reasons for doing them the way he did, and then I suggested ways to do make them better. I complimented him on how nice his classroom looked when I came to visit. How do he feel then? Was he more likely to take my suggestions to heart?

PREVENTING PROBLEMS

Many times you can avoid trouble by being on the alert and stopping the problem before it develops. Walking over to and standing near a child that is about to start mischief, all the while continuing with what you are saying, can often defuse the situation. There are several ways to deal with incipient infractions. Here are some suggestions:

Having the child alone while talking to him is vital. He has no one to show off to, so he is more likely to react appropriately.

THE FOUNTAIN FOCUS:
WHATEVER WORKS!

Sometimes problems can be taken care of by a simple physical adjustment however the teacher's attitude makes all the difference. Take the case of Patrick who is talking to his neighbors and has only two problems done on his paper. Listen to one teacher's reaction.

"Patrick, look at this! You have only finished two problems! What have you been doing? I'll tell you what you have been doing. Talking to everyone around you, that's what you've been doing! You're a real motor mouth! Now, you march yourself right up here and sit by my desk where I can keep an eye on you. You'd better finish that paper by the time the bell rings, or else! Now, get going!

How does Patrick feel? Is he going to cheerfully work hard on the problems so he can be finished by the time the bell rings and make his teacher happy? I don't think so...Either he is humiliated that the teacher has announced to the class how little he has done or he already has the reputation of being a goof-off, and this is a good way to annoy the teacher and be the class show-off. Either way, he will not be inclined to work hard to finish before the bell. Nothing will be accomplished!

You, on the other hand, walk over to Patrick's desk, look at his paper and quietly say, "How are you doing, Patrick? Only two problems done? Oh, I'm sorry. Are the kids here bothering you so you can't get your work done? Why don't you move over here where it is quiet and no one will disturb you? (smiling while pick up his books and moving them to a quiet place, possibly near your desk) You can get your work done here so you won't have to do it for homework. I'm sure you have other things to do this afternoon."

Patrick is glad to take the role of the "distractee" rather than the "distracter." You have made it clear that you are serious about his moving away from the other children, i.e. moving his books, and you have told him that what isn't finished must be done for homework. All this has been done with a smile, and he has saved face in front of his classmates. Now, he probably will complete some, if not all of the problems.

Here is another scenario. You have bus duty. Michael is pushing and cutting in line so he can get on the bus first. Instead of yelling at him, you go to him and say, "Michael, please come here at the front of the line and stand by the door. I want you to make sure that no one in line pushes.
He is now an authority figure. No one had better push in line under his watchful eye! He hardly notices that he is standing where the teacher can keep an eye on him and that he will be the last one to board the bus.

Some days even the best techniques don't seem to be working. You are taking the children to gym and Matthew just can't seem to handle himself, no matter what. You go over to Matthew, take his hand in yours and walk hand in hand to gym. You hold his hand firmly, smile at him, and pointedly hand him over to the gym teacher. Most upper elementary grade students are not fond of having to hold the teacher's hand in front of their peers. You have not said a word, but the silent subtext is there. When you act like a baby, I have to treat you like one.

ACP DISCIPLINE METHODS

One of the most helpful courses that I could write for the ACP "Continuing Education Courses" was on discipline. I wanted to expose my students to many different kinds of classroom control. Some had posted rules and when a child misbehaved, his name was written on the board. I had my candidates perform role-play classroom scenarios. Every time they repeated the infraction a card was placed on their desk. When they collected three cards on their desks, punishments were meted out. Other plans gave prizes when the class earned so many points for being good.

These are the 4 P's of the Fountain FOCUS Discipline Approach:

In private,I asked the child to tell me what happened. I then acknowledged his feelings about it. (warned about pattern)

1. I asked if his response to the problem was profitable for him, that is, was what he did a good idea? The child usually replied in the negative. If he did not, I talked with him until he agreed that what he did was not a wise course of action. (reinforced protocol)

2. I asked him what he thought should be done about it. I would not accept an, "I dunno." I pointed out that it was his problem and he must come up with a fair penalty. The solution must satisfy both him and me. (reflected about performance)

3. When we both agreed on a solution, I had him write down what happened and what he would do to rectify the problem. This was his contract with me. He dated the paper and we both signed it and filed it in a safe place. (performance contract)

4. We carried out the discipline. If the misbehavior was repeated, obviously his solution didn't work. If the solution worked, I told the student how proud I was of them. (Praise!) If it did not work, I called the child back and we went through the steps again finding another solution. (Repeat Steps 1-4} like wash, rinse, and repeat!)

ROUND ROBIN CLASS MEETINGS

Once in a while there was a class-wide problem. Sometimes there was a problem on the playground and everyone was upset or one child in class was causing a problem for everyone. It is time for a R. R. class meeting. I set certain rules for class meetings and everyone would sit in a Socratic circle.

The first part of the meeting was spent stating the problem and how it made us feel. One child would talk at a time. An effective way I found to control this was to toss a stuffed "stress apple" to the speaker. While she or he was holding the squishy apple, no one else could speak. Then when that she or he had finished talking, the speaker tossed it to someone else. When we had exhausted the topic, or when I felt that there was nothing new to add, we moved on to the second part.

The second part was spent in thinking of possible solutions. If the child who is causing the problem was in the class, I was very careful not to let it be a "rumor spreading" session where the whole class picks on a certain student. The student was allowed to respond to the class' comments, then we tried to think of a way that we could help the offending student improve. It had to be done with a feeling of goodwill. This is a situation in which the attitude of mutual respect, begun on the first day of school, paid off.

NEW STUDENT

When we had a problem with children being unkind to someone in the class, on a few occasions I used this "thinking" activity in my classroom that was extremely successful. This had to be used judiciously, because I knew that by recess the entire school would know about it.

I told the children that we were going to have a new class member. We would create her or him. I asked the class what characteristics they would like to see in a new class member. I asked them to describe the person. We drew his/her picture (in one case, they couldn't decide, so they created twins!) on a piece of drawing paper. Everyone in the class got an opportunity to add something. We talked about what kind of person the new member was.

Then, unexpectedly, I began to make disparaging remarks about the "new class member" using expressions I had heard the children use. Suddenly, I snatched up picture that the class had created, wadded it up in a ball and threw it in the trash.

The children were stunned! They asked me why I did such a thing. Because everyone had a part in creating this new class member, they had invested a good amount of emotion in the imaginary person.

"Oh, do you want to keep him?" I asked. They all agreed that they did. So I went to the wastepaper basket and took out the picture. I made a perfunctory attempt at smoothing out the wrinkles, then gave it to the students and told them to smooth the wrinkles out. They tried but of course, the wrinkles couldn't be smoothed out completely.

Then I talked about how once you have said something hurtful, you can never un-say it. The wrinkle you have caused is permanent. On more than one occasion, a child has volunteered that they were made to feel just like that paper – just a piece of trash to be thrown away.

THE FOUNTAIN FOCUS:
WHATEVER WORKS!

I found these to be very workable solutions to discipline problems in my classroom. They allowed me to keep a good rapport with the children when I had to discipline them.

Chapter 14

LEARNER FRIENDLY ENVIRONMENTS

The environment we create for our students is equally as important as the content we teach and the learning strategies we use. This applies to all teachers of all age groups from preschool to graduate school. The environment includes the atmosphere, the traditions we set, the furniture arrangement, the centers or special areas within the room, and the decorations. All of these things add up to create either a positive or negative environment for students.

Here are some tips to help you in creating a welcoming environment:

♦ Students feel welcomed and inspired to learn from the moment they walk through your door.

This can be accomplished in a variety of ways. Primary and elementary teachers may want to decorate their door with a theme. It can be a simple welcome theme, your classroom theme, or a unit theme.

Some examples might include:

- Welcome To Your Special Place
- Blasting off to Learning
- Come Explore Learning in Room 409
- Come Be High-Flyers With Mrs. Fountain

THE FOUNTAIN FOCUS:
WHATEVER WORKS!

Middle school and high school teachers may not want to decorate their door with a theme, but can use other items to show students that their room is a place of caring and learning.

Some examples:

- Special artwork done by students
- Artifacts that show your personality
- A welcome statement of some sort
- A class pledge, song, or slogan

When setting up your room, first do a sketch to get an idea of how everything will look and to help you stay organized when moving everything around.

Ask yourself:

- ♦ Should I use rows or groups of desks?
- ♦ Should I use tables?
- ♦ Should I have a reading corner
- ♦ Should I have a special place for centers?
- ♦ Should I have a time-out area?
- ♦ How easily will I be able to move between students?
- ♦ Can we all get out of the classroom quickly in case of an emergency?

Classroom walls and bulletin boards are covered with thought-provoking and stimulating material.

- ♦ Motivational posters inspire students. Every beginning of the school year, I cut out all capital letters to go around my entire classroom with this saying: "you can do anything that you put your mind into doing!"

- ♦ Primary classroom walls should be language rich with words and pictures

- Some posters can be practical such as listing classroom expectations, or things to do when finished early.

- Humorous posters tell students you know how to laugh.

- A poster of good manners and/or life skills is good to have up for reference during a teachable moment.

Bulletin Board ideas:

- Quotable quotes

- What's New—to post classroom, school, community, and world events
- Birthday board

- Centers—Use a board to post brain challenges or learning center activities

- Miss Manners

- Famous Authors (Do Not Forget About Me…I love to visit classrooms!)

- Who's Who is Room ___ (spotlight students & their work)

- See what We're Doing—post student work

- Theme—changes with each unit

- Famous Scientists

- Careers

- Famous Mathematicians

- Highlight a concept being taught

- Who Am I?—show a baby picture and clues. Students have to guess who that person is.

I Will:
Listen
See
Speak
Feel
Think
Reason
Read
Write

I will do all of these things with one purpose in mind:

To do my best and to not waste this day,
for this day will come no more.

Chapter 15

CLASSROOM MANAGEMENT PROFILE

REMEMBER: It is important for the substitute teachers to establish their classroom expectations and consequences at the beginning of the day. It is essential for teachers to be perceived by students as secure, as being in charge, and as being fair.

Remember that every individual student is a person who deserves to be treated with respect regardless of his or her intellectual abilities, primary language, social training, cultural background, or personal situation. Students respect adults who respect them.

It is extremely important for the teacher not to lose their temper or control of their emotions. Teachers should model appropriate behavior even under highly stressful situations. When teachers lose self-control, it becomes more difficult to make proper decisions and to retain the respect of students. When teachers lose self-control, their behavior often becomes the FOCUS of attention rather than the student's behavior.

Direct eye contact and non-verbal communication are effective classroom management tools, provided that the non-verbal communication doesn't become threatening or intimidating to students.

Using different voice inflections in the classroom is appropriate only if it has a legitimate educational purpose, doesn't result in yelling (which is ineffective and abusive), and doesn't demean students.

Letting the entire class know what your expectations are is key to having a successful educational day. "Establishing high standards" should be done as early in the day as possible. Teachers need to be firm, fair, and consistent. Setting reasonable standards and consequences and consistent enforcement of these standards is essential in maintaining a safe and orderly learning environment.

Students need to understand that if they chose to follow or violate classroom expectations, a correlation exists between their choice and the consequence. Negative student consequences should be logical and in proportion to the seriousness of the violation. Rewards should also be in proportion to students' correct choices. Rewards should have a legitimate educational purpose, and the reward offered should be sufficient enough to motivate students to want to continue making correct choices.

Students, like adults, respond to positive reinforcement better than to cynicism or use of the negative. Praising desired behavior is much more effective than punishing undesired behavior. Preventive discipline is more effective than reactive discipline.

It is more powerful and appropriate to correct students one-on-one at every grade level. Students who are corrected in front of their peers often respond by acting out even more. Often the student who is being publicly disciplined will have their peer group rush to their support at the expense of the teacher. A general guideline at the elementary level is "to correct privately and to praise publicly."

Students need and expect clear direction and predictability. Clear direction and teacher predictability provide a safer and more secure learning environment for students. A disciplinary surprise is usually not only ineffective; it often results in the students perceiving the teacher as being unfair and unreasonable.

Proximity & Classroom Management: There is a direct correlation of distance of the teacher from the student and student behavior. The closer a teacher is to a student, normally, the better the student's behavior. Teachers who walk around the classroom and monitor student conduct usually maintain much better classroom control.

Unoccupied and non-directed student time often results in classroom management difficulties. Teachers should provide learning activities for students to begin working on immediately upon entering the classroom and upon concluding their regular classroom assignments.

Minor unacceptable student behaviors are often best dealt with by using Fountain FOCUS techniques. These usually result in minor unacceptable student behavior disappearing. If the undesired behavior persists, the teacher will need to use more direct and vigorous disciplinary intervention strategies.

Students usually find it important that their parents/ guardians endorse their behavior at school. In most cases parents appreciate their children's teacher letting them know how their child is doing at school. Teachers will usually find parents helpful in encouraging their child to make proper educational choices when notified. When parents believe that the teacher is sincerely concerned about the welfare of their child, they are almost always willing to be supportive. It is equally as important to let parents/guardians know when their child is doing well.

Unless the educational activity dictates, generally no more than two students should be out of their seats at one time. Normally, students should not be allowed out of their seats when the teacher is doing large group instruction or is working directly with the student's assigned group.

Teachers should never intimidate students with consequences that they are unable or unwilling to deliver. Teachers who make these types of threats are setting themselves up for frustration and failure. Teachers should clearly spell out consequences of student choices and then be prepared to back up their words by consistently enforcing the consequences.

Students will generally recognize fair and rational rules and consequences when they know that the teacher is genuinely concerned. Students should not be singled out or used as an example. When a teacher has had to repeatedly or strongly correct a student, it is important that before the student leaves for the day, that the teacher reinforces with the student that they care about them, believe in them, and sincerely want what is best for them. Teachers need to role model terms such as please, thank you, excuse me, etc.

It is imperative to listen carefully to students and to consider their point of view before disciplinary action is taken. Listening to students is particularly important when there is a situation where the teacher may not have all the information. The process of listening will not only assist the teacher in making proper decisions, but will often result in a teachable moment for that student.

The ability to call students by name is a very powerful tool in classroom management. The use of a seating chart can be helpful in helping the substitute teacher to call students by their names.

It is difficult to identify in advance appropriate disciplinary consequences for every circumstance that might arise in a school environment. Generally, substitute teachers should plan on utilizing the regular classroom teacher's rules and consequences. Usual disciplinary consequences include: name on the board, loss of a privilege, loss of free time, a call to the parents, keeping the student after school. Remember to check on bus transportation, and make sure that the parents/guardians have been notified in advance and have given their permission before this option is used. A referral to the office usually comes only after other disciplinary strategies have failed to bring about the desired result.

Chapter16

CONSTRUCTING A CLASSROOM ENVIRONMENT

CLASSROOM ENVIRONMENT WORKSHOP (EXCERPT):

Managing a classroom can really establish how your year will go! Students like to know that the teacher is in control and knows exactly what is planned for the day. When teachers tell their students what is expected of them, students are able to rise to those expectations. Having a high outlook will than carry over into the students' work and the teacher will be able to do more individual and group work. In every well-managed classroom the teacher is able to because it is a successful learning environment.

Every teacher gives their classroom a very personal touch to the room and that creates a great learning environment. As a teacher you want your classroom to say "welcome to my relaxed classroom, make yourself at home" because your children will not feel intimidated. The classroom should have some fun objects that help get the kids interested in learning.

Every classroom is arranged differently depending on the size or shape but the most effective classroom is the one that permits you to "get to know the group" according to D. L. Fountain. That means that if you run a classroom that does a lot of group work you would probably have your desk in clusters. A classroom should be easy to move around in and support all of your students needs. Even if you think you have a great room arrangement and you find out on the first day it is not working so you end up changing it until it works for all students. It is very important for children to be comfortable in their learning environment.

After the environment of your room is figured out and your students understand your rules and expectations your next job is to figure out the most effective way to implement them. The classroom needs to be set up in a way so that the children have easy access to books or other materials used. It is a good idea to have the materials used more than three times a week in easy access places and other materials put away. By doing this you will save class time because the students know where things are. Teachers should model good organizational skills for their students because that is really how students learn. Students should not be expected to keep a clean desk if their teacher is unable to do the same. As a teacher you have many papers to keep track of and having a filing system could help. Having a folder for each subject may help you keep from misplacing assignments. Teachers should also encourage students to keep assignment notebooks because they tend to forget about all the homework from the different subjects. One good idea is to have the students show their parents the assignment notebook and initial it so the teacher knows the parents are being informed of their school work. Keeping the grade book and lesson planner organized can be a tedious job for anyone. Staying organized can make your day and year a lot less stressful if you know exactly where everything belongs and you put it their.

Another major problem in school is all of the transitions children have to make. In middle school students are going form one classroom to another every period and this can be very hard on both teachers and students right away. It is a good idea for teachers to develop a routine so that when students come into the classroom they know what to expect. According to the Fountain FOCUS Discipline Approach, "Teachers who make abrupt transitions, flip-flop and become stimulus bound will experience discipline problems and general disruptions." There are a couple of ways you can created a smooth transition; you can inform your children of the lesson the day before, give them a five minute warning before you end one subject and move on to the next. Basically, if you understand your children and what they respond well to than you should be able to create smooth transitions.

Rules are very important to have because it set the frame work for the classroom. As a teacher it is a good idea to pick no more than ten rules for students to follow or they will never remember them. Ten rules may even be too much; maybe just have generalized rules that cover other rules. Teachers need to have some rules to follow because it will help them be more consistent. Some rules I may follow someday are: staying organized, encourage cooperation, hold positive expectations, communicate clearly and concisely, give children choices, be consistent, forgive and forget and my favorite is using natural and logical consequences for discipline. As a teacher you want your children to feel safe and comfortable in the classroom so setting rules and enforcing them with all students is very important. Remember, " if your rules are not congruent with your personality and teaching style, these rules and their warnings will come off phony, the students will sense that these are not your rules, and these rules will eventually become ineffective".

Classroom management can be tricky for teachers and can change every year depending on the students. It is very important to have an effective classroom that supports your children emotionally, physically, and intellectually. Most importantly though they need to know what you expect from them in the classroom so they can meet those demands. As a teacher it is your sole purpose to know and build a relationship with each child so that they can learn as much as possible while in your class. On our midterm one of the questions asked was, "Of all variables what has the largest effect on student achievement?" the answer was classroom management.

Chapter 17

SPECIAL LESSON TO ENCOURAGE SELF-WORTH

The goals of this chapter are that, after reading these valuable words, you will understand reinforcement theory and develop strategies to use reinforcement theory as part of your classroom management plan.

On this page you will find three parts to the lesson: (1) introduction; (2) motivation; and (3) identifying the behaviors you want. A forum center assignment follows.

Component 1—Introduction

All teachers, whether they are in their first year in the profession or veteran teachers encounter discipline challenges. As we make every effort to build relationships with students and foster an atmosphere beneficial to learning, we need to have some understanding about what influences student behavior. The first concept of student behavior is:

Students choose their behavior!

As teachers, we know that life experiences and other factors may influence the choices students make, and we know we can't control what happens to students outside of school. But knowing that students do make choices about how they act allows us to try to influence the decisions they make about how to behave.

Component 2 – Filling The Void

People live in collective groups and in a school setting; it is important that students find their place in the classroom community. The idea that someone fits into a group is based on the feeling that they are successful in that setting. It is important that the person also feels linked to other people in the group, which might be the teacher or one or more of the other students in the room. Finally, people feel they belong when they believe they have something of value to contribute to their group. Teachers use many strategies to help students feel competent, connected and respected in the class.

Component 3 – Five Goals

Interest
Authority
Retribution
Escaping Failure

We have all worked with students who misbehave to get attention, either from the teacher, their classmates, or sometimes from their parents. Although teachers sometimes indicate frustration about giving some students more attention than others, this is not about fairness, but rather, it is about a student need. In some instances, students perceive negative attention to be preferable to no attention.

Students may also misbehave in an effort to gain power over themselves, sometimes the teacher, and on occasion even over the entire class. Creating a climate where power is shared between the teacher and the students, through offering choices and other strategies, helps some students feel the sense of power they need.

In cases where misbehaviors are based on a need for revenge, students often lash out at people who are unrelated to the situations that are hurtful in their lives. Children with problems at home may come to school and "take it out" on the teacher, or another child in the classroom.

Component 4—Escaping Failure

Students often indicate that it is easier to look bad than it is to look dumb. Misbehavior gives the student some control over a situation where he or she feels helpless because of lack of skills or knowledge.

If we are able to identify the goal of a student's misbehavior, we can more effectively respond to immediate situations as well as interact more purposefully with the student over time. We are not able to change a student's behavior since it is a choice on their part, but we can influence their choices.

Think about some of the students you have worked with in your classroom. What would be some indicators that would allow you, as the teacher, to identify the goal that is driving a particular student's misbehavior?

In a typical classroom there are usually three groups of students and they tend to fall into the following categories:

80% of the students hardly ever break the school rules. They come to class motivated, ready to learn, and able to understand and conform to the rules established in the room. These students do not need a discipline plan as they intend to match their behaviors to school expectations.

12% of the students break rules on a regular basis. These students need an understandable set of expectations and consequences to help them manage their own behavior and prevent them from disrupting learning for others.
8% of the students are unremitting rule breakers.

As teachers, our job is to devise a discipline plan that will manage the 12% without over controlling the 80% and will allow flexibility for dealing individually with the 8%.

As you think about the students in your classroom, you may know a student who is in the 8% category in one classroom and an hour later is in the 80% range for another teacher in a different subject area. This student could be FOCUSed and on task in a math class with all assignments completed in an efficient manner.

This same student could be quite disruptive in a social studies class with lengthy reading and writing assignments. Could this change in behavior be interconnected to academic strengths and weaknesses of the student? Could it be the instructional styles of the teachers in the classes? Is it possible that one teacher is more skilled at building relationships such that the student is able to feel more associated in one class than in another? Careful examination, watching the effects of consequences on the student and looking for patterns of behavior in many school settings can be helpful in trying to figure out what the student needs in order to succeed in working with teachers and other students.

MOTIVATION AND PROTOCOL ESTABLISHMENT

People select their behavior, and they frequently make their choices based on the consequences and responses of others to those chosen actions. In the classroom, teachers use reinforcement strategies to influence the choices some of their students make. Thinking again about the 80-12-8 profiles, many of your students come ready to follow your directions and learn. However, some of the students don't have the same intrinsic motivation to participate in academic endeavors as others, and rely on extrinsic factors to help them make their decisions.

Reinforcement theory isn't just for K-12 students; it applies to adult students and non-students as well. Think about what motivates you to get to work on time. Is it the calm feeling you have because you don't need to rush and will have time to review your lesson plans before the start of the day, or is it because your supervisor would be annoyed, or because your colleagues might make a comment if you came in late?

While I was a graduate student taking classes at Nova Southeastern University, some students completed all of their tasks early and enjoyed the stress-free feeling of knowing that nothing is hanging over their heads, while others waited until the middle of the night, just before a project is due, to complete each lesson. For some people, the strain of the deadline, imposed by the instructor, helps them prioritize their time and energy.

Jot down some things you would continue to do whether or not any one ever noticed. Next list a few things you might stop doing right away if there were no negative consequences for not doing them. Finally, write some things down that you would not continue to do if they were ignored and you received no praise, thanks or other positive reinforcement for having done them.

There are times when we may find ourselves shifting from the 80% mind set, actions guided by intrinsic motivation, to the 12 % mind set, where our choices are guided by extrinsic rewards and/or the ability to avoid or eliminate negative consequences put in place by others. This was true with my students as well. A student, named Matthew, may really enjoy academic assignments and complete all of his schoolwork on time, but hates to participate in physical education activities. The only reason Matthew would ever sign up for a Physical Education class would be that it is mandatory for graduation and his diploma would be withheld if he did not take the class. Another student, named Kerstin, loved sports, especially basketball, and hated doing assignments for some of her classes. She may need the guideline of a minimum grade point average for players to be eligible to play on teams in order to give her the incentive to turn in her work on time. A third sample student, named Josh, on the other hand, may feel satisfied with getting C grades in school, but may develop a great relationship with one of his teachers and work hard enough to get an A in order to receive that particular person's praise and approval.

Reinforcement is neither good nor bad; it is simply a fact that some of our behavior is influenced by the ways other people respond to it. As teachers, we construct behavior plans to increase the likelihood that students will perform in certain ways in the classroom and complete school work in a certain manner. Let's look more in depth at what it is we may want to reinforce, and how to increase and decrease specific behaviors.

PERFORMANCE CLASSIFICATION

When you are developing conduct program, it is important to know what behaviors are important in your classroom and what you currently do to:

1. Generate a culture for learning,
2. Prevent discipline problems from taking place.

Let's look at strengths and needs from two perspectives.

Here are three questions to ask from the teacher perspective. First, what do you feel you do well? Is it easy for you to get students engaged in conversation? Do you have a good sense about how you give directions? Do students usually begin work quickly after you have assigned them a task? Do you connect with parents quickly if you anticipate a student may have a problem with behavior? Can you use wit to deescalate a problem? Think about some areas where you feel successful and write down a proposal or a plan that has worked for you.

Second, in what area would you like to improve? This could be something like getting students' attention more quickly or designing group work so everyone shares liability for tasks. If you are working with young children, it could be shortening the time it takes to get ready to go home at the end of a school day. When you reflect on your day, where are the aggravation points? This may help you zero in on areas to modify.

The third question to ask yourself is what do you need for your classroom to run well? This will vary from teacher to teacher based on their style and the developmental level of the students they teach. If you do a lot of small group work, perhaps you need your students to know how to assume roles and take turns. If you give students a lot of independent assignments, perhaps students in your class need to know about distributing resource materials and putting them away so they can be relocated effortlessly.

Now, let's ask the same three questions about the students you teach:

- √ What do your students do well? Have you found that they are regularly willing to contribute ideas in discussions? Are they paying attention to what you teach such that motivation is not a worry? Do you find that the students in your classes are helpful to each other?

√ What do your students need improvement in? Do your students really struggle when trying to solve problems with peers? Is it difficult for them to take turns during classroom discussion? Would they be learning better if they could ask for help when they are unsure of instructions for assignments? What students need to improve is influenced by the ways you teach and the expectations you hold for them to thrive in your classroom.

√ The third question, "What do the students need?" is also important to ask. If there is a wide range of academic abilities within the classes you teach, some may need modified and/or extended assignments. Some children may come from competitive home environments with a great deal of pressure to excel in all areas. Those students may need help in dealing with stress. In other situations, there may be little or no support for some students to complete schoolwork outside of the school day. Students in an advanced chemistry class may need very different things than students in general music. Likewise, children in an accelerated math class may have different needs than those in a remedial reading group. That will influence how you manage each group of students.

BEHAVIORAL PATTERNS AND MODIFICATION

When we think of positive reinforcement, we are identifying desirable consequences that follow a behavior and cause the behavior to repeat. Each person determines for himself or herself what is desirable, so we cannot always tell what is serving as reinforcement for a behavior. However, if the behavior continues, it is probably being reinforced. Reinforcement can come from within or without. One person may choose to dress a certain way because they like the way they look, while another person may dress in a particular manner because of the comments they receive from others – ask me why I prefer school uniforms?

"One student may consider a trip to the principal to be a punishment, while another student may see the attention as a positive experience."
- D. L. Fountain

Many students are intrinsically motivated to work efficiently in school. They see and understand the benefits of educational work and behave in a supportive manner, following the teacher's directions. However, school is work and sometimes it is necessary to use extrinsic reinforcement to continue a setting where students put forth their finest effort. External recognition and rewards are not bad; they serve to influence our motivation to do things. Teachers love their work, but few would continue to do it without a paycheck every two weeks.

As we think of consequences, they fall on a continuum from very much in the control of external forces to totally in the control of the person receiving them.

At one end of the scale, there is the stuff we use to influence the choices other people make. This is proven and is easy to see and touch. Money, food, toys; stickers, etc. fall into this grouping. Stuff can be given to a student in a very restricted manner. An acceptable answer on a math test can equal one piece of candy, or five dollars can equate to every A on a report card.

Further along the scale, closer to intrinsic motivation, is a category of opportunities. This might include time to visit with friends, choosing a place to sit in the classroom, spending time on the computer, recess time, etc. In these cases, the reinforcement is not as easy to touch and the person brings some choice and control to what they get from the experience.

Closer still to the internal incentive is a class of rewards called social recognition. This type of reinforcement is less tangible still, and students decide what value they place on the recognition. These types of recognitions can include praise, honor rolls, a call home, etc. In these situations, there is nothing to touch, necessarily, but the recognition can definitely influence student behavior.

PRAISE, Praise, and give more Positive Praise!

Confidential and personal, individual recognition
Confidential, group reward identification
Public, individual detection
Public, group acknowledgment

The developmental level and age of the student can influence which setting will work best. Kindergarten and first grade teachers often use public individual praise to influence the behavior of other students.

Observations like " I like how Michael is standing so quietly in line" sends a message to Michael that he is doing a good job, but it also tells the rest of the class to look at Michael and behave like him. This works well for many elementary grade teachers, but would probably not have the same success rate with high school students.

For many adolescents, the goal is to not be singled out in front of their peers; so many expert middle school and junior high teachers use confidential, individual and private, group settings to deliver praise and recognition. Try these tips in your classroom. If it doesn't work, use a "Whatever Works!" approach. Do not give up yet!

Anything not understood in more than one way is not understood at all.

Chapter 18

LEADERSHIP BEHAVIOR IN THE CLASSROOM

While I was a Principal, I devoted a great deal time to helping my teachers understand the essence of the problem called "the number-one restriction to our educational process." I offered theories for why previous attempts at solving classroom discipline problems had failed and discussed the strengths and weaknesses of existing literature on the subject.

I included lots of first-person student accounts about why kids act out in our classrooms. At first, the complaints, excuses, and explanations are merely interesting—if somewhat irritating. After a while, the my faculty and staff realized that they were crucial to the understanding of what might be going wrong in his or her classroom.

I incorporated responses to what is debatably the most significant question for teachers to ask: When is a discipline problem not a discipline problem?

"A discipline problem," I stated, "is a pattern of behaviors that disrupts the learning of the rest of the class or the function of the teacher." The following are not discipline problems:

- Guidance problems, which require individual psychological intervention;

- Educational problems, which should be handled through grading or better motivational techniques;

- Personal disruptions that annoy the teacher but are not disruptive to teaching.

I called these particular situations "discipline problems" because of the way they were handled. Teachers must be able to recognize discipline problems, deal with them, and steer clear of miscalls.

SOURCES OF DISRUPTIVE BEHAVIOR

When I had conferences with brand new or veteran teachers regarding discipline problems in their classrooms, I always briefly but thoroughly discussed the four general sources of disruptive student behavior:

- Outside the classroom—such as family situations, peer relationships, and even adolescent physical development.

- Within the classroom environment—such as the general physical environment, seating arrangements, and routines and procedures.

- Involving student-teacher interaction—including miscalls, phoniness, inconsistency, inappropriateness, and unfairness.

- Related to lesson-plan delivery—such as content that is not " effective," experiential, inductive, or interactive.

PREVENTING AND HANDLING DISCIPLINE PROBLEMS

When I was asked to speak at a conference, I really enjoyed delving into the nitty-gritty of classroom discipline. I discussed specific "SMART" strategies for preventing discipline problems by addressing the sources of those problems. Some contributory factors cannot be altered. "You cannot avert those problems that happen from just growing up or from home or from associations with peers. However, you can foil a ripple outcome onto the rest of your class. I believe this with all of my heart that you can work on handling those troubled students better." I offered my staff many examples of typical classroom situations caused by factors outside the control of teacher and offered suggestions for dealing with them.

More important, however, I explained how my teachers could address the sources of disruptive behaviors that arose from problems with student-teacher interactions. I feel that these five guidelines are essential to providing discussion and examples designed to help teachers:

- Avoid miscalls
- Be authentic, or congruent
- Be consistent
- Be appropriate
- Be fair.

The other informative sections of my book include detailed information on establishing and enforcing class rules, handling punishments and offering rewards, and learning to resolve conflicts. I provided very specific information on how to deal with a number of classroom discipline problems—from students who “call out” to students who carry weapons. In my twenty years of being in the education field, either as a teacher of administrator, I have dealt with both ends of the discipline spectrum. Although geared for teachers in middle and high school, my book includes sections for elementary school teachers.

Chapter 19

STUDENT TEACHING IN 1985

I went through the Duquesne University School of Education "Teacher Preparation" program. I graduated with a Bachelor's degree in Education in 1986. I knew that I wanted to be a teacher when I was in the 8th grade.

I was in Mr. J's 8th grade class at St. Robert Bellarmine (Grades 1-8) Catholic School. I switched classes with Sister Janet. I sat in the front of his class and noticed that he used to tap this big, shiny ring with a "D" on it. On the last day of my 8th grade year, I went up to Mr. J and gave him a hug. I asked him about his ring. He said that he had always wanted to be teacher and he graduated from Duquesne University. I told him that I learned so much from him. I also informed him that I would go to Duquesne University and become a terrific teacher just like him.

I graduated from East Allegheny High School in Pittsburgh, Pennsylvania. Afterwards, I did pursue an education major at Duquesne University. During my four years, I was the cheerleading captain, joined an educational sorority (Kappa Delta Epsilon), and founded my own Women's Social Club (Mynx) on campus with the help of Father Nesti, who was the President at that time.

While I was the cheerleading captain, we were responsible for the half-time basketball shows at the Civic (now Mellon) Arena. The Duquesne "Dukes" were having a half-court shoot out to win a car. Well, I was in my senior year at the university and student teaching. I already signed a teaching contract with Palm Beach County School Board to teach 4th grade for the following school year in West Palm Beach, Florida.

I was in the middle of the arena and announcing the line up to shoot the half-court shots. I was also handing the basketballs to the contestants while handling the microphone. I looked up at the fifth person in the line. Guess who it was?

It was none other than Mr. J!!! I went over and introduced myself to him. I let him know that I was graduating with my Bachelor of Science degree in Education in the Spring and I had already secured a teaching job in Florida. In the Fall, the Palm Beach County School Board had come up to Pennsylvania to recruit new teachers. I told him that I was going to achieve my goal in becoming a terrific teacher "just like him" and he was the "spark" that started all of my educational dreams! He began to cry and so did I…into the arena microphone! The entire arena audience had heard everything that we were saying to each other. We both received a standing ovation! That was one of the BEST moments of my life!! Talk about Teacher-Student Feedback…(ha-ha).

I student taught in the Pittsburgh Public School District. By far the most important thing that I wished I had known was how vital it is to set up classroom restrictions or limits early in the school year. In part I had thought that being a "nice guy" and trying to set up a wholly positive reinforcement teaching style would work well. I was wrong! I did something about it too. You have to find the teaching and discipline style that works for YOU! I believe in a "Whatever Works" approach for everybody in the teaching profession. If it doesn't work for you, change it right away!

WHAT I BELIEVE:

I now believe that the maturity level of many of the students necessitates that there exist a threat of negative consequences as well. Truly, if necessary it is better to use this negative reinforcement as early as possible. In my first couple of years of teaching in Florida, I very much wanted to be remembered well by my students. Though not in and of itself a bad thing, letting this goal hold sway over me in the classroom hurt my teaching. It was TRIAL AND ERROR! It made me a timid about addressing some classroom discipline issues, the most prominent being the classroom noise level, people's complaints about group work, and the practice of some students coming late and leaving early. That is when I began my quest for the "effective" discipline approach.

During my first two years, I waited until problems became intolerable, and found it very hard to change without the negative feelings that could have been avoided had I taken care of things early. The problem with this was that I did not feel like I could use many of the threats and/or other incentives, so I began creating the Fountain FOCUS "Whatever Works" Discipline Approach.

I also wish that I had been more demanding up front. But, in my 3rd year of teaching I had obtained a job with Broward County School Board. I had a fantastic principal, Mr. Willie J. Dudley. Yes, he let us make our own mistakes but was there to help us design our own classroom solutions. I still keep in touch with this wonderful man! He had a "Open Door" policy for his office. We could visit with him at any time and he would help us figure things out, especially the new teachers. He was the reason that I went on for my Master of Science degree in Educational Leadership at Nova Southeastern University and later on became a principal.

Most of what I've written so far includes ways that I could have done a better job teaching. There is one more thing, which, had I believed it at the beginning of the semester, would have made my experience a better one. Many students believe that their academic success is overly tied to their instructors teaching abilities. Over the past 20+ years, I have taught almost every grade level from 1st through college level. Especially at a university level in the end students are truly the people responsible for making sure they learn the material and for the grade they receive.

My Priceless Advice For All Instructional Levels:

FOCUS IDEA #1—Do not change your plan without one week warning. If you have plan and announced that you will do something, then keep it.

FOCUS IDEA #2—They crave to pass the classes or courses. You may assign hard work or extra problems to promote your office hours or something else. They will complain at the beginning, but they will do what you assign. Follow the curriculum guides or the syllabus.

FOCUS IDEA #3—Do more than one midterm or frequent tests. Use the first test as your warning. Show your students what you want to see on the test paper. They will follow.

FOCUS IDEA #4—Do individual care. Memorize students name as soon as you can and use their name in the class. If some students are not doing well, you may e-mail their parents or them. Whatever you do, just let them know you are paying attention and genuinely showing concern for them.

FOCUS IDEA #5—Some students complain so much during the class time. If you think you have one of those belligerent or irritable students, ignore what they are saying. You must know how to say "NO!"

These are the things that I have learned from teaching and being an administrator in the educational field for the past 20+ years. I take my educational career very seriously. I wish that I could have been shown a guide like this when I was starting my teaching career. Yes, I had all of the educational foundation courses, but you do not know until you're in the trenches daily. I know that my book will help beginning and veteran, along with traditionally and alternatively certified teachers alike.

Chapter 20

TEAM EFFORT FOCUS

The Fountain FOCUS Discipline Approach includes several techniques including the "TEAM EFFORT" method. The TEAM EFFORT method is at once both very simple and very sophisticated. At its simplest it means dividing the class into 3 or 4 teams who then compete with each other. Winning is based on team contribution in instruction and individual and group behavior. The teams are competing for rewards that encourage [cluster] peer pressure: getting to leave first, getting to sit where you wish, getting extra recess time, etc.

This brief synopsis is somewhat analogous to describing baseball as simply "hitting a ball out to the field and see how the team works together to retrieve it." In reality this system is as simple or as sophisticated as is needed to match your students. I have utilized this system has been effectively used with students ranging from kindergarten through adult education. The basic principles remain the same; only the performance varies according to the level of the student.

At its heart is the use of 2, 3, or 4 teams to bring about positive peer pressure. (I always felt that 4 TEAMS worked for my classes.) Students become a part of a team, with ensuing responsibilities. It is no longer the class against the teacher. It is instead one team against the other and the teacher is the facilitator.

Rather than being a behavior management system on the side, in case it is needed, the TEAM EFFORT method is an interactive part of the classroom, with students actively participating in instruction in order to win points, and ultimately rewards, for their team.

One year I had the worst class I have ever had in my entire career. There were very few "well-behaved students," and those were easily overwhelmed by students who "seemed not to care" and instead loved the attention their inappropriate behavior gave them. I was truly shaken—and I was definitely not a first-year teacher! As soon as I got one student settled down, another would "start up" on his "I'll show the teacher" routine.

Out of desperation one day, I told the class that I was immediately dividing the class down the middle of the room and that whichever side was the better behaved would leave on time, and the other side would remain for one minute of their break time so that we could discuss how they could do better tomorrow. I asked a "ringleader" on each team to be a captain/floor manager, for their team.

Instantly things got better. All of a sudden, anyone who tried to show off was frowned on by the rest of his teammates. It was no longer cool to bug the teacher, because no matter how insignificant school work might seem, missing even a minute of breaktime was indeed significant.

I slowly refined the system so that the students had increasing ownership. I also learned to keep it simple so I would keep using it. I named the two teams the Door Team and the Window Team, which was incredibly uncreative, but extremely easy to remember from class to class.

WHY THIS SYSTEM WORKS FOR TEACHERS

This is a very powerful behavior management system using the psychological principles which make peer pressure so powerful, no matter what our age. These principles make us the social creatures that we are: (1)—we want to be liked, (2)—we want to be respected, (3)—we want to be proud of ourselves. This is just as true of kindergarten students as it is of you and me. The only thing that changes is the level of sophistication through which we seek the above.

This system also works because it no longer means "the class versus the teacher." Rather it is now "team versus team" with the teacher as both coach and umpire.

BEHAVIOR MANAGEMENT: YOUR ULTIMATE CHALLENGE

Most of us have seen a teacher near tears, distraught at how to manage a student's behavior. It's easy not to have a behavior management plan in the midst of all our other classroom demands. Often when I am explaining this system to a fellow teacher, it will sound so complicated and time consuming that he will say to me, "But I just want to teach!" And of course that would be fine if all students "just wanted to learn." But they don't.

Once, while talking with another teacher, I asked, "What if I'm a student in your room and I throw paper at someone—what would you do?" The teacher looked at me and said, "I'd tell you to stop!" I then asked, "What if I did it again?" At that point, he hesitated for a moment and said something along the lines of before, only a little sterner. I then ask, "What if I did it a third time?" He replied, "I'd write a referral and send you to the office."

Realistically, that teacher is teaching students that for the first two incidents there is no real penalty, and that they can get by with a lot as long as they only do it twice. Often any real effectiveness of the above warnings depends on how mad the teacher gets. Thus the teacher has paid a high price in terms of emotional stress, and has demonstrated to students that anger "solves" problems.

At times, a teacher may be told that "if your lessons were only good enough, you wouldn't have any real behavior problems." That's not true. Too often students with behavior problems are looking for entertainment, rather than education, or may be too needy of the attention their misbehaving brings. Misbehavior is inevitable. And it should be expected, and routinely dealt with, just as our society does with ever present parking/speeding tickets.

WHEN AND HOW TO BEGIN

This system can be implemented anytime during the year, but ideally during the first weeks of school, before the newness of the year starts to wear off. I easily spend a good part of the first month of school integrating this into my curriculum. Every lesson is a chance to practice.

5 THINGS TO REMIND YOURSELF AS YOU USE THIS SYSTEM

1—I am in charge, not the students. I am not domineering or dogmatic, but I am in charge.

2—My mental health, and my ability to enjoy my teaching, are more important that any single student in my room. I must care about my needs as a teacher first, so that I can then care about my students' needs.

3—I must have a systematic behavior management plan. Without it I rely on emotion (stern looks, threats) which drives a wedge between me and my class. My class is a mirror—what I do is reflected back at me through my students.

4—I will be consistent and unemotional in using my plan so students know what to expect. Much like a courteous policeman: "Here's your ticket, have a nice day!"

5—My ultimate goal is not for students to like me, but for them to respect me and their classmates. (Liking usually comes naturally when students see that you are consistently fair and firm.)

6 THINGS TO REMIND STUDENTS AS YOU USE THIS SYSTEM

1—No teacher is strong enough to control a class all by himself and teach effectively at the same time. If I become too busy managing behavior, I will not be able to teach, and you will not be able to learn. We must work together to have a strong class.

2—I am strong in my absolute commitment to making sure that no one keeps us from learning.

3—In this class we use positive peer pressure to help each other behave, as we might use cooperative learning to help each other learn. It's not fun to deal with a peer's behavior problems, but we are a team and we must help one another.

4—My job is not to react emotionally to problems, but simply to calmly issue a warning when appropriate. (The class will happily remind you of this part!)

5—One of my jobs, and yours, is to point out all the little things that people do to help our class, each day.

6—Sometimes I may move you to a different seat. It may be that you can provide strength to that table or team. I will keep our two teams balanced, with both leaders and followers.

WHAT TO DO ABOUT INAPPROPRIATE BEHAVIOR

This system is very simple. A student does something inappropriate? He is given a warning. He does something else? Then he is given a second warning. Two warnings during the same class equals one demerit.

A demerit must be "worked off" by copying a "list of rules for solving behavior problems," or a list of textbook definitions, or whatever might be useful for a student to become more mindful of. It's much like copying sentences, only a little more educational. But it needs to be about equal to the front and back of one page of paper so as to be somewhat labor intensive.

This is a very mundane, non-creative penalty and purposely so. It's like a traffic fine. I don't have to give it a second thought. The students know that I won't get upset—it's so simple that I can concentrate on teaching. "Here's your ticket, have a nice day."

HOW TO DISCUSS BEHAVIOR WITH THE CLASS

Students need to know that we all operate at different levels depending on the situation: explaining the rules of a game=ADULT level, playing the game=CHILD level, telling someone not to play the game in the street=PARENT level.

I often use this if I need to discuss behavior with the class: "When I was standing up here giving instructions, what level was I at? (ADULT) And what level were you at? (ADULT) And when someone threw that paper across the room, what level was that person at? (CHILD) And what level did I have to go to when a gave them a warning?(PARENT) And while I am telling you this and you are listening, what level are we both at? (ADULT)"

Students often think that because of their age they are always at CHILD level. The levels have nothing to do with one's age, merely one's responses. Also CHILD level is not inherently bad. If a family goes to an amusement park, hopefully everyone will be at CHILD level, young and old—that's how we have fun. This concept teaches students to move easily to whatever level is appropriate.

This Parent/Adult/Child concept is especially powerful for analyzing misbehavior in front of the class. Problem students often love the attention they get from disrupting the class. By analyzing their disruption publicly, as above, I am able to discuss the situation in very "scientific" terms, without even mentioning any students by name. Very quickly they get the unpleasant message that "if you are going to be disruptive—in front of the class—it is very possible that the situation may be analyzed—in front of the class.

HOW TO ORGANIZE THE TWO TEAMS

Students rarely pick seatmates based on productivity. Social considerations are far more important. Students must understand that you use a seating chart to make sure that both teams are productive and competitive, that students who are strong or weak, in terms of behavior, are equally spread between the two teams so that the former can be leaders, and the latter are relatively isolated from each other. Telling students upfront that this is your procedure and rationale helps students to accept the procedure.

From time to time you can show the class what a "wonderful" person you are by allowing free seating as long as they don't strike out. "Bobby's not working, that's strike one—Someone's passing a note, strike two.—One more strike, and we have to move back to assigned seats." Or you could let the team with more points have free seating. There are many ways that you can allow students to see the "wonderful" side of you.

TEACHER ACCOUNTABILITY:

I have had the opportunity to teach from one end of the rainbow to the other. I have taught kids who represent suburban schools, and inner city schools. I have taught both honors and remedial classes. I know that "all children can learn." I believe that every teacher should be held accountable: for teaching effectively and enthusiastically, as judged by peers and administrators, regardless of the challenges presented.

I know that "measured outcomes" vary according to the student's support system. I know that too often the stereotypical suburban student comes to school already nourished and determined to learn, whereas the stereotypical inner city student often comes to school hungry for whatever nourishment and confidence the school system can instill. Some schools have an abundance of students highly motivated to learn, other schools do not.
I know that no home or neighborhood environment can be an excuse for failure or lower expectations. But I know that learning is harder for the student who didn't have breakfast that morning, who can't afford the brand-names advertised on TV, or who is wondering which parent has custody this week-end, or whose mother got home from work at midnight and couldn't

help with homework. But in spite of all the incredible situations with which students must contend—in each situation, teachers should be held accountable: for teaching effectively and enthusiastically, as judged by peers and administrators, though the path for some teachers, and some students, will be easier.

I know that every teacher effects the "measured outcomes" of each student, but so does each parent, each friend, each neighborhood, and so does each movie and TV show. Teachers struggle daily with how to teach those students lacking the motivation to learn or the desire to achieve. Indeed, "it takes a village to educate a child." Holding only teachers "accountable" is fashionable in times when it is unclear how to hold the parent and society "accountable" for their impact as well.

MAKING LEARNING RELEVANT:

Effective learning requires the ability to see, as both teacher and student, the importance of what is learned. As a language arts teacher, I found that even though it is an especially important subject, students will only master it if it has relevance to them and their future. And so, I didn't teach just a subject—I also taught students, and I taught them in the context of a real world which requires basic concepts and skills in order to pass standardized tests, and fill out a job or college application. It is in this real-world context that students begin to see why any subject matters.

My classroom was really a combination of the fundamental (grammar, vocabulary, research) and the inspirational (poetry, prose, debate). Neither component is any good without the other. A teacher's role, as an academic guide, facilitator, and coach, is to make learning relevant for each student, whether dealing with the fundamentals, or the inspiring CREATIONS THAT follow.

Chapter 21

REINFORCEMENT OF APPROPRIATE BEHAVIORS

FOUNTAIN FOCUS DEFINED:

An undisciplined class can prevent us from doing a good job and result in wasting both time and effort. An orderly classroom creates a feeling of accomplishment where learning can truly begin.

Everyone needs a consistent protocol!
- D. L. Fountain

Your students and everyone, for that matter, need routine for a feeling of protection and security. They like knowing they can go to an environment that is safe where they can learn. To be undisciplined is to put too much responsibility on the child to guide himself. As a result they are not happy and their only thought is to quit coming to church as soon as they are old enough. A child will perform up to the expectation of the teacher therefore a teacher needs to be sure in her own mind what her expectations of her students are. Most children are mimics. They will do exactly as you expect, so the students in your class need to know exactly what is expected of them. Spell out a few simple rules for class behavior on your first class meeting. Be sure that your students understand them and that you enforce them. Remember that your students need to be reminded of your FOCUS Discipline System (Pattern, Protocol, Performance, and Praise!!!) from time to time.

Successful FOCUS Discipline:

Children need the security of authority balanced with a happy and friendly attitude in their classmates. Every behavior has a payoff. Proper handling with even the very smallest child is most important for this reason. The success of your class depends upon good discipline.

> *Good discipline contributes to a happy, pleasant and efficient learning environment!!*
> – D. L. Fountain

If the payoff is desirable, the behavior continues. If it is undesirable, in time, the child discontinues it. A child learns by trial and error, and by observing the results of his efforts and the reactions of those around him. Most children respond to love and to our positive acceptance of them. They want to please. Never tolerate bad behavior. Handle it immediately. Physical disciplinary action such as spanking, slapping etc should never be used in the classroom setting. A kind and positive way of handling children will get the best results! A simple "No" or "Please do not do that again" can accomplish much.

Certain PROTOCOL must always be followed or else there can be no control in the class. The teacher must use a firm, but calm tone of authority. Believe me, my classes knew that Mrs. Fountain did not play around when there was work to accomplish! I would take charge whenever the group needed me. But, to humanize myself to my students, I often sang or hummed around my classroom. Sometimes humor can rescue you too…I liked to tell "education" jokes in my classrooms too. Never talk down to a student – no matter how old she/he is – I always used "treat others the way you want to be treated" in every class that I taught from Pre-K through College Level. Use the same tone of voice and amount of respect that you would give to an adult. Children, after all, are also individuals and they have an incredible insight.

ELIMINATING THE DISTURBANCES IN YOUR CLASSROOM:

Discomfort, disturbances and disorganization can cause inattention among the students in the classroom. Discomfort from unsuitable furniture, uncomfortable chairs, poor ventilation, extremes of temperature, bothersome wraps, inadequate lighting for reading should be considered. Most of these factors can be overcome. Another reason for inattention comes from disturbances such as intrusions by latecomers or conversing teachers. It helps to be aware of this and to strive for punctuality. A disorderly classroom such as: competing sights and sounds, teacher's mannerisms, unorganized teaching materials, or pictures above eye-level can all lead to either daydreaming or boredom. These things can be changed.

CHALLENGE YOUR STUDENTS:

A teacher's goal is to challenge students at their current level of knowledge and to get them to move beyond it, to a higher plane. However, sometimes you sense restlessness, tenseness, and tiredness in your group. Remember that children, especially boys, approaching adolescence and growing rapidly have difficulty sitting still. Twitching muscles and jiggling legs are symptoms of their age. Try to teach the children to "wiggle" quietly. Have quizzes and games that include memory work and reviews that will help strengthen the students listening skills. The result is that everyone can learn and benefit. I always adjusted my material to my daily classroom atmosphere. You must be thoroughly prepared. Ask appropriate questions. Use the children's names to keep them alert. Gestures or lively facial expressions can be appealing. When you manifest enthusiasm it usually demands that your students maintain order.

PROTOCOL MAINTAINS CLASSROOM ORDER:

Another way that the teacher can maintain order and keep the children's attention is by having consistent protocol. I know you have heard me say this before – but this is very, very important! Consistent Protocol!! These rules must be enforced and followed. Sometimes a simple touch, word of encouragement or an invitation to help can open up the shy, withdrawn or introverted child. Discover his interests that will lure him into participating. Commend him for his efforts. Whereas the child who bites, kicks, pushes, destroys or boisterous and does not respond to the positive and various methods of encouragement and guidance to channel his energy into acceptable patterns should be quietly and firmly separated from the group.

ESTABLISHING THE PROTOCOL

ALWAYS, Always, always, let the students know immediately your expectations and make them very high!!
- D. L. Fountain

Tell the students during the first class your expectations concerning their behavior, preparation, punctuality, homework etc. The rules should include behavior such as: children talk only when called upon by the teacher or when their hand has been answered; children remain seated and get up only with the teacher's direction; children keep their hands to themselves; children from primary class up go to the washroom before they come to class; children listen quietly. Every rule must be policed, enforced and monitored. If it cannot be enforced it is NOT UNDERSTANDABLE!

PROTOCOL SYSTEM NEEDS TO BE SIMPLE

Children need to be aware of what they cannot touch or do in a classroom. Don't allow eating or drinking in the classroom, unless you think your class can handle it, and it might already be a school rule – check it out! Instill a consideration for others by keeping the noise down when walking or talking so as not to disturb other classes. There are some rooms that have elements of danger in them. Rules need to be made because of safety factors. These can vary from one class to another and should always be explained. Don't allow the children to rock backwards on their chairs or sit on the tables. Rules also need to be made because younger children are limited in their responses and abilities to handle all equipment, like scissors.

CHECK YOUR PROTOCOL SYSTEM

Obviously there should be more rules for children in lower grades than in higher ones. Even so, it is wise to make only a few rules at a time, firmly establishing them before you introduce others. Maturation is fundamentally the process of learning to discipline one's self. From time to time check your rules to see if the students have outgrown them.

GREET EACH STUDENT!

Greet each child pleasantly as she/he arrives in your classroom. Avoid commenting on awesome clothes, all children do not have the same opportunities. Be Fair and Steady! Try not to shower some with more attention than others. Try to find something worthy of praise in each child. Don't single out favorites. As they leave the class, tell them how good they were. Make all praise genuine.

FOUNTAIN FOCUS HINTS FOR PRE-K:

Don't allow parents of toddlers into the classroom to stay with their children on a regular basis. It doesn't seem to matter how long that "mother" goes in with them—separating doesn't seem to get any easier. Only if little ones have a fear of staying alone, encourage the mother to stay for a few minutes, or as long as it takes, rather than let the child leave with her. The latter can become a habit and other children can become quick to realize that they can cry to leave with their mothers. Some children feel more secure with adults than with other children even though they have left their parents, be prepared to hold them on your lap or close to you if necessary. The clinging child should be encouraged and rewarded for leaving the teacher to join the group. One effective method for the nursery age child is to simply put happy faces on their hands, one for coming to class with a happy heart and the second one for behaving in class. It works! Also, it provides the parents with immediate knowledge on how their child was in class. Another excellent remedy for crying children is to place a facial tissue, cotton ball or a Band Aid in his hand. He is immediately distracted and rubs his eyes to see what he has been given. The result is obvious. Follow this up with an interesting activity.

For the small child seating arrangement is very important. They should always be in a position where you can reach them comfortably and unobtrusively to touch them. The sense of a gentle touch on a little hand or arm portrays a feeling of love and understanding and gets their attention in a pleasant way. It will usually do one of two things: the child who likes to be touched will leave his arm where you can touch him again, or, the child who does not like to be touched will sit back very well and attentive hoping you will never do that again. Either way it accomplishes the same end!

Encourage the younger children to go to the bathroom before going to the assembly area, explaining how it disrupts the services when children go in and out. The assistant in the young classes should help with the washroom visits.

FOUNTAIN FOCUS HINTS FOR ELEMENTARY LEVEL

Classroom control begins as soon as the child leaves his parents to enter class. In a large building there should be someone to police children as they go through the hallways and up or down stairways to the classrooms. The children should be expected to behave quietly and respectfully at all times. They can enjoy the pictures you have up, the things on the interest table, room, decorations, etc; but they can also understand that running and noisy play is not acceptable at this time.

For orderliness each child should have his own chair with his name on it, in the same place every time. This prevents scrambling around for chairs and the child knows exactly where he can go to sit. Have extra chairs for visitors. When there are children who bother those near them a new seating arrangement may need to be made. The teacher needs to be tactful.

Whenever possible use an activity to divert attention from being lonesome or restless to induce good behavior. The teacher has to decide whether to take the misbehaved child from the group. She must decide if he is too tired to be with other children or whether she should interest him in something new. The teacher must judge when to do something and when to leave the child alone. A change in weather or a special holiday may cause some children to be over-stimulated. Watch for the child who appears to be overly excited and lead him to quieter activities. Sometimes restlessness results from a lack of group experience. Be conscious of this child and help channel his restlessness into acceptable patterns. Involve him in conversations; commend him for effort;

let him help in some small way. Put the child's aggressive tendencies to work. Ask him to help you lead the songs or in straightening up or in passing out papers. Children love to be helpers. Ask them to get something or to help the smaller children or to point to something on the wall. This will allow him to get off his chair or move without him feeling naughty.

FOUNTAIN FOCUS HINTS FOR SECONDARY LEVEL

When the first student arrives have some meaningful activity ready. Handling a child one at a time is easier than waiting until disorder has become organized. If you are teaching for the first time, don't leave the first period blank as get-acquainted time. Children open up and are easier to handle when their attention is drawn away from themselves to something that interests them. Don't allow older children to take precious class time to tell about gifts, parties, etc. Let them know you are interested and will listen to them after worship service. Birthdays are tremendously important to children and some special recognition should be made of them, but not necessarily during class time as it takes away the much-needed minutes in the hour to teach the prepared lesson. However, a birthday card sent through the mail could be worthwhile or a small present bought for the child and given to the child separately is thoughtful.

My supervising teacher in Pittsburgh, Lynn Hohman, always told me that you couldn't get more out of a container than you put into it! My own mother always said to me that you could grasp more bees with honey than vinegar! A teacher cannot make the students care about her; instead, she must care about them, for care begets care.

Always explain to the student why they are being disciplined so that they understand what actions are not acceptable in the classroom. Let the unruly child know that there is PROTOCOL System that must be obeyed. Speak to her or him in a nice but firm, low tone while looking right into her or his eyes. Be sure she/he is aware of what she/he did wrong. Never threaten to do something that you cannot or will not carry out. Idle threats never work!!
Using the Fountain FOCUS Discipline Approach, immediately, firmly and politely will work in your classroom! If it worked for me, it will work for you! If it doesn't, then find "Whatever Works" for YOU! If a tap on the shoulder

does not alleviate the problem then do not hesitate in quietly leading the child out into the hall for a brief explanation of the proper rules of behavior. Talk to the offending older student privately after class explaining that the class learning is being disrupted by his misbehavior and it cannot be continued. If the misbehavior continues, give the student a second warning during the class period in front of the other students explaining that the misbehavior will not be tolerated. Notify the parents and the elders as soon as possible after class of the behavior problem. The student will return to the class the next session.

Get to know your students and their home life. Possibly, if you can, learn why they have a conduct problem. Every student needs to be considered: extroverted, introverted, hyperactive, shy, frightened, and naughty. Remember that each one has been prejudiced by: home, health, heredity, school, and peers. Often domestic, financial or health problems can effect the children. Sometimes a new baby in the house has made him feel left out or an older child has started school leaving him feel unimportant. Illness in the family, a new parent, lack of effective discipline or lack of respect for authority can cause bad behavior.

Teaching in 5 different states, I have found that if one of my students who get too little attention at home she/he needs a lot more from me. I was always willing to give extra attention and praise too! Once I learned what applied to each student in my class, I could handle her or him a little easier. Be prepared to handle all of your students objectively.

I have always found that if your students do not respond to you or the discipline as you expected they would, don't show your disappointment, irritation or anger; instead analyze what you are doing to see if the problem lies with you. 94% of all discipline problems are a direct result of the teacher overlooking something in the learning environment. The most inexcusable reason for discipline failure is that of the teacher arriving late. The teacher should always be the first in the classroom, and set the tone for her class by her presence. Inadequately preparing a lesson and presenting it inappropriately to the students cause most behavior problems. PREPARATION AND PROMPTNESS GOES A LONG WAY!

Chapter 22

DISCIPLINE FOLKLORE

Rewards motivate your students, no matter what grade level, to be accountable. Though, there is a fine line between motivating your students and bribing them with extrinsic items. The toy, ticket, or computer time becomes the FOCUS, not responsibility. In addition, we are not honest with young people when we give them rewards for expected behavior. Society does not give such rewards. When was the last time you were rewarded for stopping at a red light?

Usually, consequences not punishments are needed to change your student's behavior. Punishments satisfy the punisher but do not a lasting effect on the punished. If punishments worked, why are they so often repeated? Once the punishment is over, the person has served the time and has relinquished responsibility. Punishments prompt antagonism, not accountability.

In general, young people need to be continually notified what to do...If notifying worked, you would not have to reiterate everything over and over again. In fact, notifying is often interpreted as disparagement and promotes defensiveness, not conscientiousness.

Your students in the classroom do not always need bribes to be good.

1. Rewards can be wonderful ACKNOWLEDGEMENTS.

2. Rewards can be great INCENTIVES—if the person chooses to work toward the reward.

3. CON—When we give students rewards for expected behavior, we send a false message. Society does not give rewards for appropriate behavior.

CON—What comes of rewarding expected student behavior can be understood in remarks like, "What's in it for me?" and "If I'm good, what will I get?" This approach undermines the social fabric of our civil democracy.

CON—Giving such rewards does not foster moral development. Good or bad, right or wrong, just or unjust, moral or immoral are not considered. Instead the determining factor becomes getting the "prize."

"Usually, rewards along with praise for an expected performance imply that good behavior is essentially meaningful."
- D. L. Fountain

PLAIN PUNISHMENTS, NOT UNDERSTANDABLE CONSEQUENCES, DIVEST YOUNG PEOPLE OF THE PROSPECT TO BE ACCOUNTABLE FOR THEIR OWN ACTIONS.

1. Punishment moves ownership of the problem from the student to the adult.

2. Punishment is too often used for those who don't need it. These students will respond without punitive action.

3. Punishment is teacher-dependent, rather than student-dependent. The threat of punishment may coerce a student to act appropriately in one class but have no effect on the way the student interacts with others outside of that class.

4. By the time students have reached the secondary level, some have been lectured to, yelled at, sent out of the classroom, kept after school,

referred to the office, suspended in school, suspended from school, referred to Saturday school—and these students simply no longer care.

5. Behavior may temporarily change at the threat of punishment—but not the way the student WANTS to behave.

6. Punishment is temporary and transitory. Once the punishment is over, the student has "served his time" and is "free and clear" from further responsibility.

7. Punishment is based on avoidance—a negative response. It stirs feelings of fear, anger, resistance, and/or defiance.

8. Punishment in the classroom arouses resentment and invariably diminishes student motivation to learn what the teacher desires.

9. Punishment, by its very nature, is counterproductive to good teaching because punishment fails to foster responsibility, cooperation, or positive motivation.

10. The use of punishment in the classroom automatically creates an adversarial relationship between the teacher and the student.

11. This adversarial relationship oftentimes results in the student's testing the teacher to see how much the student can get away with.

12. Some young people test the limits of acceptability. Sometimes the use of authority is necessary. However, authority can be used without being punitive.

13. If you believe a 9 year-old is a 20 year-old, then you will use the same approach with the former as with the latter. However, if you believe that a 9 year-old is not yet a 20 year-old then you will help the youngster help himself.

NOTIFYING

AFTER CHILDHOOD AND THE DAYS OF OUR YOUTH, I USE THE TERM "NOTIFYING" IS OFTEN INTERPRETED AS AN EFFORT TO CONTROL.

1. Whenever we notify people how to do something differently, we convey a subtle, negative message that the way they have been performing is wrong or not good enough. This often creates defensiveness. That is why there is a tendency to resist, especially when telling involves notifying others how they personally need to do something differently.

2. Notifying implies that something has to be changed. People don't mind change as much as they mind being changed.

3. People love to control but hate to be controlled. This is especially true for adolescents who are attempting to assert their independence.

4. Notifying is related to rewards and punishment in that all three are external attempts to change behavior.

5. Responsibility can only be taken, not told.

Chapter 23

80 WAYS TO COPE WITH STRESS

1. Get up at least 15 minutes earlier
2. Prepare for the morning the night before
3. Avoid clothes that do not fit well
4. Rely on yourself
5. Set appointments ahead
6. Don't rely on your memory ...write it down
7. Practice spiritual maintenance
8. Make duplicate keys
9. Take your vitamins
10. Set priorities in your life
11. Avoid negative people
12. Use time wisely
13. Simplify meal times
14. Always make copies of important papers
15. Anticipate your needs
16. Repair anything that doesn't work properly
17. Ask for help with the jobs you dislike
18. Break large tasks into bite size portions
19. Look at problems as challenges
20. Look at challenges differently
21. Simplify your life
22. Smile
23. Be prepared for rain
24. Tickle a baby
25. Pet a friendly dog
26. Don't know all the answers

27. Look for a silver lining
28. Flatter someone
29. Teach someone to fly a kite
30. Play in the rain
31. Schedule a walk into daily routine
32. Take a bubble bath
33. Be aware of the decisions you make
34. Believe in yourself
35. Stop saying negative things to yourself
36. Visualize yourself winning
37. Develop your sense of humor
38. Stop thinking tomorrow will be a better today
39. Have goals for yourself
40. Dance an old song
41. Say "hello" to a stranger
42. Ask a friend for a hug
43. Look up at the stars
44. Practice meditation
45. Learn to whistle a tune
46. Write a poem
47. Go see a symphony
48. Watch a ballet
49. Begin a new book curled up in bed
50. Do a brand new thing
51. Stop a bad habit
52. Buy yourself something special
53. Smell flowers at grocery store
54. Find support from others
55. Ask someone to be your "vent-partner"
56. Do it today
57. Work at being cheerful and optimistic
58. Put safety first
59. Do everything in moderation
60. Pay attention to your appearance
61. Strive for Excellence NOT perfection
62. Stretch your limits a little each day
63. Look at a work of art
64. Hum a tune from your childhood

65. Drink more water
66. Plant a garden
67. Feed the ducks
68. Practice grace under pressure
69. Stand up and stretch
70. Always have a plan "B"
71. Take an art class
72. Memorize a joke
73. Be responsible for your feelings
74. Learn to meet your own needs
75. Become a better listener
76. Know your limitations and let others know them, too
77. Tell someone to have a good day in pig Latin
78. Throw a paper airplane
79. Exercise every day
80. Learn the words to a new song

Chapter 24

TEN THINGS TEACHERS WISH PARENTS WOULD DO

1. Be involved in their children's education. Parents' involvement helps students learn, improves school and makes teachers' jobs easier.

2. Provide resources at home for reading and learning. Parents should have books and magazines for their children and read to or with their children each day.

3. Set a good example. Parents should show their children that they believe reading is both enjoyable and useful. They shouldn't spend all their time in front of the TV, either.

4. Encourage children to do their best in school. Parents must indicate that they believe education is important and that they want their children to do the best they possibly can at school.

5. Emphasize academics. Too many parents get caught up in athletics and in preparing their children for the world of work, when academics should be their first concern.

6. Support school rules and goals. Parents should take care not to undermine school rules, discipline or goals.

7. Use pressure positively. Parents should encourage children to do their best, but they should not apply too much pressure by setting unattainable goals or by involving them in too many activities.

8. Call teachers early if there is a problem (not wait for teachers to call them), so there is still time to improve the situation.

9. Accept their responsibility as parents, and not expect the school and teachers to take over this job. For example, parents should make it their responsibility to teach children basic discipline at home rather then to leave this task to teachers.

10. View drinking by underage youth and excessive partying as a serious matter, not a joke. Drinking, partying and staying out late take a toll on students' classroom performance. While parents are concerned about drug abuse, many fail to recognize that alcohol is the drug most frequently abused by youngsters as well as adults.

Live a good, honorable life. Then, when you get older and think back, you will be able to enjoy it a second time.

Chapter 25

TRY THIS

Difficulty following a plan (has high aspirations, but lacks follow-through); sets out to get straight A's, ends up with F' (sets unrealistic goals.)

FOCUS TIP:
Assist student in setting long-range goals; break the goal into realistic parts. Use a questioning strategy with the student: Ask, what do you need to be able to do this? Keep asking that question until the student has reached an obtainable goal.
Have student set clear time lines, and establish how much time he or she needs to accomplish each step.

Difficulty sequencing and completing steps to accomplish specific tasks (e.g., writing a book report, term paper, organized paragraphs: solving division problems).

FOCUS TIP:
Provide examples and specific steps to accomplish task.

Shifting from one uncompleted activity to another without closure.

FOCUS TIP:
Define the requirements of a completed activity. (E.g., Your math is finished when all six problems are completed and corrected,' do not begin on the next task until the first task is finished)

Difficulty following through on instructions from others.

FOCUS TIP:
Gain student's attention before giving directions. Use alerting cues. Accompany oral directions with written directions.
Give one direction at a time. Quietly repeat directions to the student after they have been given to the rest of the class. Check for understanding by having the student repeat the directions.
Place general methods of operation and expectations on charts displayed around the room and/or sheets to be included in the student's notebook.

Difficulty prioritizing from most to least important.

FOCUS TIP:
Provide a model to help students. Post the model and refer to it often.
Prioritize assignments and activities.

Difficulty sustaining effort and accuracy

FOCUS TIP:
Reduce assignment length and strive
Increase the frequency of positive reinforcements. (Catch the student doing right and let him/her know it)

Difficulty completing assignments.

FOCUS TIP:
List and/or post (and say) all steps necessary to complete each assignment.
Make frequent checks for work/assignment, completion.
Arrange for the student to have the phone number of a "study buddy" in each subject area.

Difficulty with any task that requires memory.

FOCUS TIP:
Combine seeing, saying, writing, and doing; student may need to sub-vocalize to remember.
Teach memory techniques as a study strategy (e.g., mnemonics, visualization, oral rehearsal, numerous repetitions)

Difficulty with test taking.

FOCUS TIP:
Allow extra time for testing; teach test-taking skills and strategies; and allow student to be tested orally.
Use clear, readable, and uncluttered test forms. Use a test format that the student is most comfortable with. Allow ample space for student response. Consider having short answer tests.

Confusion from written material (difficulty finding main idea from a paragraph, attributes greater importance to minor details).

FOCUS TIP:
Provide student with copy of reading material with main ideas underlined or highlighted.
Provide an outline of important points from reading material.
Teach outlining, main idea/details concepts. Provided tape of text/chapter.

Confusion from spoken material, lectures and audiovisual material (difficulty finding main idea from presentation, attributes too much importance to minor details).

FOCUS TIP:
Provide student with a copy of presentation notes.
Allow peers to share carbon copy notes from presentation. (Have student compare own notes with copy of peer's notes.)

Frequent messiness or sloppiness.

FOCUS TIP:
Teach organizational skills. Be sure student has daily, weekly, and/or monthly assignment sheets; list of materials needed daily; and consistent format for papers. Have a consistent way for students to turn in and receive back papers. Reduce distractions.
Give reward points for notebook checks and proper paper format.
Provide clear copies of worksheets and handouts and consistent format for worksheets. Establish daily routine; provide models for., -what you want the students to do.
Arrange for a peer who will help him/her with organization.

Poor handwriting (often mixing cursive with manuscript and capitals with lower case letters).

FOCUS TIP:
Allow for scribe and grade content, not handwriting. Allow for use of computer or typewriter.
Consider alternative methods for student response (e.g., tape recorder, oral reports).

Agitation under pressure and competition

FOCUS TIP:
Stress effort and enjoyment for self, rather than competition with others. Minimize timed activities; structure class for team effort and cooperation.

Frequent self put-downs, poor personal care and posture, negative comments about self and others, low self-esteem.

FOCUS TIP:
Allow opportunities for the student to show his & her strengths.
Give positive recognition…praise!!!
Remain calm, state infraction of rule, and don't debate or argue with student.
Have a pre-established consequence for misbehavior.
Enforce rules of the classroom consistently. Design discipline to "fit the crime," without harshness.
Reward more than you punish in order to build self-esteem.
Change rewards if not effective in motivating behavioral change.

Difficulty using unstructured time, recess, hallways, lunchroom, locker room, assembly, and library.

FOCUS TIP:
Provide student with a definite purpose during unstructured activities.
Encourage group games and participation (organized school clubs and activities).

Loosing things necessary for task or activities at school or at home (e.g. pencils, books, assignments both before, during, and after completion of assignment).

FOCUS TIP:
Help students organize. Frequently monitor notebook and dividers, pencil pouch, locker, book bag, desks.

Provide positive reinforcement for good organization. Provide student with a list of needed materials and their locations.

Poor use of time (sitting, staring off into space, doodling, not working on task at hand).

FOCUS TIP:
Teach reminder cues (a gentle touch on the shoulder, hand signal, etc.).
Give the student a time limit for a small unit of work with positive reinforcement for accurate completion.
Use a contract, time, etc., for self-monitoring.

Chapter 26

THEY DON'T TEACH YOU THIS IN TEACHER PREPARATION SCHOOL

I have a list of frustrations from the first couple years of teaching, mainly things they don't teach you in a teacher preparation school: (I actually saved it – such a pack-rat!)

1. Copy machine course #1001

2. 6th through 8th graders can't walk quietly down the hall without grabbing each other, but the preK-5th graders can. Why is that? Why didn't "teacher school" prepare me for that?

3. How can you modify the curriculum so some students who need the challenge can get it (I have some students with a 115% average), and other students who need a slower paced class can have that. (I have students in the same class with 11%)

4. How to read/comprehend different teacher manuals 101

5. How to have fun with a class and not letting them "cross the line".

6. How to make modifications when an assignment is due and they need that skill to move on, but 2 were absent, 3 didn't attempt the HW, 3 left it at home, and everyone else did it.

7. How to drink water when needed from talking all day, yet manage to hold "yourself" until a convenient time.

8. How to organize students work that is:

late and graded

missing assignments

make up

graded and not in the grade book

graded and in the book, ready to go back

work that is needed to keep to work on at a later date

9. What do I do with all the memos that the school gives me?

10. It is the 4th week of school. I still don't' know everyone's name. Luckily, I am learning personalities quicker.

11. I'm a brand spanking new teacher ...actually from Pittsburgh, teaching in the sugar cane fields of Pahokee, Florida (looooong storrrrry – NO where near the BEACH!), [Palm Beach County School Board's Motto in 1985: "Come and TEACH ON THE BEACH!"] so I have all the responsibilities of being a teacher of record and also a choice of catching a teacher bus in the morning for a 2 hour (one-way) ride to school or driving the 2-lane road with live gators in the canals on both sides who are ready to eat me for breakfast and dinner. FUN!

I don't have a peer teacher or a mentor, yet my department is incredibly supportive...but sometimes I feel like a bother with ALL of my questions, as they have classes to teach and software to wrangle. I do have a friend named "Ella!" She helps me out tremendously! She gives me classroom management and other ideas when I run out of mine...when wrestling with this huge bunch!

The biggest problem I'm having is classroom management. I realize that most of it is trial and error, but I'm having a hard time judging the length of activities so that there's always something on the desk. Compounding that is the fact that I'm a 4th grade teacher, I teach 13-15 year olds, and I am not bi-lingual. I do not always have extra activities at my fingertips. Quite a few of my classes are filled with talkative students that speak different languages. I just don't feel like I'm giving enough work based on the amount of chatter I try to quash.

12. My homework dilemma(s):

Gather my students together and write the question at the top of the board:

"Why Don't My Students In Class Do Homework?"

As kids name reasons, write them on cards and tape them to the board (under the title). Try to have as many as possible. Here are a few that would likely come out:

Dance Lessons/Soccer after school

I have to take care of my siblings after school

I have to work in the fields with my parents or siblings

My parents aren't home to help me

Too much homework (2 hours plus)

I don't know what to do when I get home

Teacher assignments are unclear (so I don't know what to do when I get home)

From here I ask the kids to identify causes and effects. I draw an arrow from the cause to the effect. So for example (using the examples above):

Because I have to work or play a sport after school, 2 hours of homework is too much. I do draw an arrow from “Soccer” or “Work” to “Too much homework”

Because Teacher assignments are unclear, I don’t know what to do when I get home. I do draw an arrow from “Teacher assignments” to “Don’t know what to do”

I am surprised by the root causes that come out of my Rapport Exercise. From here I made plans with my students. I always thought that the teacher usually has a role in the problem and this is my way to try and correct things. As I said before, it is all TRIAL and ERROR! Whatever I can get to work in my classroom works for me!!

USE A “WHATEVER WORKS APPROACH IN YOUR CLASSROOM AND YOU WILL ACHIEVE RESULTS!!

Chapter 27

DISCIPLINE STORIES AND ANSWERS

A chubby **fifth-grade** boy named Arthur Lee (actually in my class) was scared; it was his first day at class, in a new school. And on that very first day, his worst fears were realized.

Hours after his arrival, several kids at his new school started making fun of him and calling him names like "pumpkin face" and "fat." Humiliated beyond words, Arthur Lee withdrew to himself and turned into a different, *lonely* boy.

But when I used my remarkable "Fountain FOCUS classroom management approach and conflict resolution method" to handle the classroom conflict, Arthur Lee later became a **confident boy** admired by many of his classmates.

Meet Tiffany.

She was a confused girl who wrecked her parent's car and had a teenage pregnancy and got an abortion without her parents knowing about it. She had a sister who seemed to do everything right. Who in fact constantly received accolades from her parents while Tiffany got cold shoulders, looks of frustration—and critical words.

After putting the Fountain FOCUS four P's of Discipline into action, Tiffany's sour attitude and reasons for acting rebellious quickly surfaced. During my sessions, her father "understood" her pain and rebellion. Finally, he gave her some of the "recognition" she *secretly* desired and the envy over her sister ended.

This terrible family problem was finally resolved...

And there's Morgan. She was a girl who seemed to have a gift for math. She always seemed to have the right answer during math class. After awhile, some of her classmates started teasing her and drove her to hide her math genius. This caused her to act differently at home. Her parents wondered what was wrong with their little girl.

The Fountain FOCUS method was applied. And now Morgan does not shy away from answering questions in class and excels at math. Her classmates now praise her for her mathematical prowess of which they were once jealous. (Morgan's parents couldn't be happier.)

The Sabans were an interesting **family with five kids.** As you can imagine, there were major battles between the kids.

Utilizing the Fountain FOCUS approach, all five children learned to *work out* their conflicts in a productive manner that gave the parents blessed relief from the squabbling.

Christine was fast approaching what looked to be the start of anorexia nervosa, a serious eating disorder.

Both her and her mom **fought like cats and dogs** over eating, clothes, TV, going out, just about everything you could think of. Home life was an environment riddled with stress.

Using the Fountain FOCUS approach, I brought to the surface the "real" issue that was causing these endless battles between Christine and her mom. After applying the 4 P's of Discipline, the Fountain FOCUS, her mom and Christine, for the most part no longer revisited this issue.

And then there's Raymond.

His dad, recently divorced had married another woman. Now Raymond had a **step mom he resented** taking orders from. Fights erupted in the home. And Raymond's dad and step mom were at their wits end as to what they should do.

By applying the Fountain FOCUS approach, Raymond started acting much better and most of the "non-stop fighting" and "hard feelings" ended. There was contentment and peace in the home again.

And these case histories are just the tip of the iceberg!

That's why I know the Fountain FOCUS approach is exactly what you've been looking for to gain more control in your classrooms, halt the fighting and unlock more peace and delight into your classes and with student rapport.

Because without it…and I know this is a bold claim to make…those dreadful fights and blood pressure raising scenarios between you and your students will persist with no conclusion in sight.

Chapter 28

SHARING OUR UNIQUE KNOWLEDGE

The majority of my ideas are probably already being used in some districts:

- Provide sufficient time – including teacher-designed structure/ guidelines

- Set an expectation that sharing will occur.

- Encourage peer observations (make possible by hiring substitutes, providing "administrator certificate" for class coverage, etc.)

- Provide Peer Coaching Training.

- As a component of staff development, require teachers to present at staff meetings (new ideas, information obtained at workshops/ conferences, ideas that have immediate application potential, etc.).

- Implement a Peer Support System for all teachers.

- Implement "Curriculum Day" – Example: several districts whose teachers were incorporating a new math program paid those teachers a stipend that enabled them to meet after regular school hours to share/ discuss their experiences. Such a model could be extended to other disciplines, provided funding is available.

- Hold Parent Evenings/Forums – could be with content area or grade area teams.

- Provide forum for teachers to share student work/projects.

- Have teachers teach courses to other staff members – include a mechanism for those taking the courses to obtain credits or CEU's – again, funding may be an issue.

- Use staff meetings only for the purpose of discussing teaching and learning issues – find another forum to deal with "business" issues.

- Devise chat-rooms, bulletin boards, or websites that permit/ encourage sharing.

- Encourage teachers to be presenters at workshops/in-service days.

- Encourage teachers to apply for SEED grants.

- Investigate sources of grant money that encourage teacher creativity and attach an expectation that the project will be shared with fellow teachers– i.e. PTA funded grants, district Mini-grants.

- Share classroom successes through district-wide newspapers.

- Ask teachers to videotape lessons or parts of lessons – make the tapes available to fellow teachers.

- View all classes as equal in importance.

- Implement a built-in continuing contact model.

- Incorporate a Critical Friends Groups model.

- Use teachers as skills resources – devise a resource bank and encourage/require teachers to contribute to it.

- Create/implement an in-house Teacher Academy based on best practices.

- Incorporate a "Behind the Glass" model for classroom teachers.

- Provide teachers (content area or grade level teams) with common office space, time, and support.

- Train teachers on sharing protocol.

- Remove "barriers" to teacher growth.

- Encourage team teaching – includes finding resources that permit this to happen.

- Administrators should model appropriate sharing.

- Provide daily team time (by grade level or content areas).

- Participate in workshops with other schools (2-3 times per year).

- Administrators need to be cheerleaders/promoters of teacher successes – i.e. at board meetings, etc.

- Promote teacher/ed-tech coordination.

- Increase sabbatical opportunities for teachers (contractual issue?).

- Provide stipend for teachers to serve as Learning Results facilitators.

- Form a Teacher Leadership Council – a function would be to disseminate information to other tea chers.

- Schedule "specials" back-to-back – may help to provide common time for content area teachers.
- Include regular early-release days into the school calendar – work in own schools or with others.

- Extend the teacher year (workshop/in-service days) for the purpose of improving/sharing.

QUESTION 1

HOW MIGHT WE FOCUS EVALUATION ON STUDENTS' STANDARDS-BASED LEARNING?

- By using local/classroom-based school assessment to drive instruction and discussion of progress toward goals.

- Identify at pre-conference how they plan to carry out their plans to meet specific professional goals. How are goals that aren't met addressed?

- Include a self- evaluation as part of this process.

- How does a teacher FOCUS on specific learning outcomes? What types of assessments are needed?

- Not about teacher performance but about student learning—What is the evidence of student learning?

- A variety of assessments will certify student learning.

- Evaluation is continual, not snapshot, sometimes outside of classroom instruction.

- Lesson plans aligned with Learning Results and student understand what it is?

- Students need to know standards before test/assessment.

- Develop baseline data to use to analyze performance over time "growth factor."

- Develop teacher evaluation system to include evidence of teaching towards learning results.

- How teachers rationalize their assessment results in terms of linking to standards-based learning.

QUESTION 2

HOW SHOULD THE EVALUATION PROCESS BE ALIGNED WITH STAFF DEVELOPMENT?

- Link the teacher individual goals to yearly professional goals and building and district goals.

- Evaluate how staff development is used.

- Evaluation should be a two way street. An administrator should learn from individual staff evaluation process what the overall building needs and priorities should be.

- How does evaluation enhance student learning?

- Review and discussion of school assessments for class and school weakness.

- Use of a rubric for guidelines dealing with school and district wide professional development.

- Staff having a complete understanding of what the standards are.

- Teacher involved in the evaluation process throughout self-analysis of their teaching and goals. Identify weakness.

QUESTION 3

HOW MIGHT THE EVALUATION PROCESS ENCOURAGE BEST PRACTICE?

- An ability to teach drives improved student outcomes

- Teacher need for reflection drives change

- Ability to accept and use feedback

- Critical friends/peers to encourage reflection

- Need multiple measures to assess long term growth

QUESTION 4

WHAT WOULD YOU ACCEPT AS EVIDENCE THAT STUDENTS ARE LEARNING?

The information gathered to answer the reflective questions could be divided into two categories:

- Student Portfolios

- Teacher Professional Portfolios

Suggested parts of a student portfolio that might be used for supervision and evaluation of educators:

- Student ability to communicate about learning
- Student ability to reflect on needs and set goals
- Demonstrations of a variety of learning styles and assessments
- Applications of knowledge

Suggested parts of a teacher portfolios:

- Analysis of student scores
- Development of long term plans
- Samples of lesson plans
- Established link between student work and the reporting system
- Willingness to modify program for individual student needs
- Goals reflect assessment data
- Willingness to change
- Commitment to Lifelong Learning
- Capable use of data to reflect, develop and change
- Clear communication skill

QUESTION 6

HOW SHOULD STAFF EVALUATION LINK TO STUDENT LEARNING?

For new teachers, administrators should rate the new teacher on how she/he "understands/uses variety of formal and informal assessment strategies to evaluate/support the development of the learner."

There are four (4) "domains" of effective teaching. (They are: Environment, Instruction, Planning and Professionalism...with each area having a sub set of indicators).

- Utilize a "team" approach to set whole-staff goals and use valid data to improve instruction and assessment practices.

- Include a "self-reflection" piece.

- Include a "student input/feedback" and a "parent input/feedback" piece in all teacher evaluations.

- Use non-threatening language Eg. Instead of "Does Not Meet," consider a phrase like, "Exploring Now."

- Have a rubric-based way of rating each standard Eg. Needs Improvement, Exploring Now, Proficient and Distinguished.

- Use student work in the process of any administrative or peer process.

- Administrative visits should be frequent, but short, with longer visits planned for specific purposes, connected to indicators or goals.

- Administrators need time and training in use of these kinds of tools / protocols.

Chapter 29

PARENTS CAN CAUSE PROBLEMS

Parents' actions cause discipline problems too. I believe that teachers need to be aware of and address the other causes of discipline problems before addressing this one. The other causes of discipline problems are more under the teachers' control. If they are taken care of, often parents, even difficult ones, will not be a negative factor in the educational process.

There are several types of parents to deal with who cause discipline problems. They are the ones that are most predisposed to their children's complaints about the school setting and the classroom. Most parents with complaining children would probably be astonished if they could see their children's actions in the classroom.

Some parents are alarmed with their children's complaints, but when they come in for a consultation and can see that the report is not precise, they can acknowledge reality and work things out. Often times their concerns stem from the unfortunate educational experiences of their own childhood and they feel that they want to prevent their children from having the same type of experience.

Still, other parents are the ones in deep denial of problems concerning their own interaction with their children. The relationship problem most apparent to the teacher is with parents who cannot discipline the child. Then the school organization becomes the scapegoat for any behavior problems. In the younger grades the answer may have been that the schools aren't teaching them how to behave. By the time the child reaches high school and the child's behavior is less suitable in the classroom, the parents utterly refute that the child has any behavior issues that they need to address and control. They go to great lengths to challenge the school behavior policies rather than plainly tell the child not to do that certain behavior – Pattern, Protocol, Performance, and Praise (4 P's of Discipline).

In my opinion, the mistake that parents most often make is to furnish the child with a specific type of complaint that will defend the child in being discourteous, insubordinate, disrespectful, or unruly to the teacher in the classroom. Once children learns the magic language that will allow them to act as they wish, they will simply lie about the teacher and classroom situation, or they will maneuver the teacher into a behavior that somewhat resembles the magic expression behavior that excuses disrespect, etc.

While I taught in California, I talked to a parent about a student who was rude and defiant in a study hall because I was insisting that the student be quiet and study. I phoned the father and his response was, the child felt singled out for rules that no one else had, and he wasn't being heard. The father said this as if justifying his child's behavior in the above situation. My answer was that the rules were uniformly enforced, no one talked without permission and when they did, they studied together quietly at the front of the study hall. I added that his child had furiously told me that he, his father and myself were going to have a chat about this. I told the father that I was not going to discuss about whether or not a student should be quiet in my study hall without the vice-principal involved and that if he wanted a meeting about that, he should contact the vice-principal. The outcome of this discussion was that the student would be quiet in the study hall and no further meeting was held. However, teachers should be aware that if I did not have clear rules which were stated and fairly enforced from the beginning of class, and had a working relationship with the vice-principal, the results of this episode might have been much different.

While I was teaching in Florida, a parent complained to the principal and to the superintendent because I would not give credit to a student because the parent claimed that a lengthy European vacation was an educational equivalent to the unit that the student had missed a significant part of and needed to make up. Because the complaint was not reasonable in the school setting, it did not result in any further action on my part.

While I was a Principal, a parent complained that one of my teachers had used excessive force because her child had brought an open pop container repeatedly into class. Short-and-sweet, the school rules were against it. In reality, the student had stood outside the classroom until the bell rang to begin class, and then he left and went to the soft drink machine and came back seven minutes later with his soft drink in his hand and a smile on his face. That complaint was followed up with a meeting with the child, parents, the teacher and me. In the meeting I explained and proved, because I had documentation, that this was not a new situation, which the student had been told before, and that finally if he did it again, he would be sent to my office. I supported my teacher, and there were no further incidents that school year, but the child should not have been led by the parents to think that they would justify that type of behavior.

In one other incident, earlier in my administrative career, both parents came into office demanding a meeting with me regarding one of my teacher's actions in a class. In this conference I realized when the parents said that this type of behavior was seen in their child's classrooms through the years, I knew that the parents had practiced this routine many times. They felt the dilemma could be solved with an adjustment in the teacher's behavior and not in their child's behavior. A light bulb went off! I further realized since my teacher was not in error and the parents were not going to see any reason. I supported her and I wanted to make this a comfortable experience for everyone involved. From this incident, I learned that the principal is only as good as their teachers and staff. I don't know that the parents or the student learned much from their side of the situation. The student continued on undisturbed, with far less than optimal educational growth.

For teachers who are in the middle of the demands on the classroom teacher: papers, planning, meetings, goals, standards, student needs, and parent conferences, there is perhaps no time for learning the psychology of parent behavior. I wanted my teachers and staff to know that they were professional, competent, and knowledgeable about those parents who cause discipline problems in their classrooms. I always supported my teachers when they were dealing with these types of situations. I made sure that my staff and I had the necessary training to recognize and deal with those parents whose children are disrupting the education of the rest of the students.

Chapter 30

WAYS TO SAY "NO"

That's not an option

I am unwilling...

Say it in a funny way, i.e. "Never in a million trillion years!"

Sing, no, no, no!

That's not appropriate.

I am not ready for you to do that yet. (Great for teens)

For a younger child, use distraction Ask, "What do you think you would need to do before I would be willing to say yes to that?"

Ask, "What do you think?

Is this a good choice for you?" (If you choose this, make sure you are willing to abide by her answer)

For a youngster that has something you don't want him to have say, "That's not a toy."

Ask, "What are your other options?"

No, but I would be willing to...

I appreciate your asking, however…

Walls are not for coloring. Here is a piece of paper. Tell them what to do instead i.e., "Water needs to stay in the tub."

This is not negotiable

Can you come with another solution?

Chapter 31

STUDENT HOSTILITY

Over the last 20 years, I have taught mainly in urban school districts. During my fourth year of teaching in south Florida, I had some trouble with a few students who exhibited vicious tendencies in class, such as verbally intimidating other students or myself and throwing a book against the wall when upset. With my background, this is what you need to do to prepare for next year to avoid similar problems.

Student violence is a serious concern all around the state and the nation today. Regardless of whether a school district is rural or urban, small or large, issues of student violence and discipline may exist anywhere. Each school district in the state is required to adopt and post a student code of conduct. The code of conduct minimally must establish the standards for student conduct in the district and must specify the circumstances under which a student may be removed from a classroom, campus or alternative program. Additionally, it must outline the grounds for suspension or expulsion in accordance with state law. When a student has violated the code of conduct, a teacher is required to report the violation to the principal or administration. This "report" is often referred to in school districts as the discipline referral form.

A teacher may remove a student from the classroom and send him or her to the office under two scenarios. First, a student may be removed from class if the teacher has documentation of repeated interference with the teacher's ability to communicate with the class effectively or with the ability of other students to learn. Second, a student may be removed if his/her behavior is so disruptive or abusive that it seriously interferes with the classroom environment. The primary difference between the two scenarios is that continuous documentation is not necessary under the second because the behavior is probably a single occurrence (student throwing desk across the room) versus multiple acts over time (persistent talking, refusal to follow directions, etc.)

A teacher must remove from class a student who engages in any conduct that would automatically require the student to be removed to an alternative education program or expelled. The conduct may occur either on school grounds or while attending a school-sponsored or school-related activity on or off school property. Acts requiring student removal, but are not limited to, conduct punishable as a felony, assaults, terrorist threats and the sale, possession or delivering of drugs and alcohol. The student may either be suspended for up to three days or placed in an alternative school. Acts requiring expulsion include the use or possession of a firearm, aggravated assault and arson.

Under either type of removal, the principal may not return the student to the removing teacher's class without the teacher's consent, unless the placement review committee determines that it is the best or only placement available. The Admission, Review and Dismissal (ARD) committee must review requests for removal of special education students. The ARD committee must determine whether the behavior in question is related to the student's disability. If the behavior is related to the student's disability, the student may not be removed from the regular classroom. If the behavior is not related, then the special education student may be treated as any other student for discipline purposes.

Each teacher should be sure to review his/her district's code of conduct and the campus or district discipline management plans for information on how specific discipline issues are to be addressed. Documentation of discipline problems is of the utmost importance and you should be sure to follow the district's instructions for making discipline reports.

Learning is a treasure that will follow its owner everywhere.

Chapter 32

ADVICE FOR ROOKIES

One of my ACP teachers was having trouble in his class. The students would not listen to him, they were very talkative, and loved to talk back while he was teaching. I made several trips out to his school to observe what was going on. He really struggled to keep his cool. He was getting upset easier and extremely frustrated. He told me that for the first two weeks his students did really well, but now they had some problems.

Here was the situation, as it stood right then!!! From what I saw, there was very little effective teaching and learning occurring in his classroom. In the early months of this, your first year, he had been getting good results. We were at mid-year and his students have "figured him out". They had clued into what they could get away with…almost anything!!! He could work 16 hours a day preparing lessons and still, everything would seem futile. He had so much that he wanted to give but the little folks just weren't receptive. They were not attentive and many of your hours of lesson preparation seemed to go down the drain. The students were unhappy! You were unhappy! They felt it! You felt it! You go home every night totally exhausted and feeling VERY depressed. You've still got lots of love in your heart for your students, but that's diminishing quickly, especially with the serious discipline cases. Soon, parental complaints will begin and you will have those additional headaches with which to contend. As I mentioned previously, I've been there…done that! MANY teachers have!!!!!!!

Every good teacher MUST develop "effective classroom management skills." Without them, a teacher hasn't got a chance! Today's kids don't walk into a classroom and behave automatically. They must become convinced that behaving is much better than misbehaving. It's very easy for teachers to say that today's kids are wild and spoiled and out of control, and impossible to teach. It is true that today's kids are MUCH TOUGHER to manage. However, they are still MANAGEABLE!!!!

I told him that he was the ADULT (and the surrogate parent) in your classroom, and the only one! How goes you, goes the class! Give the kids an inch, and they'll try to take a mile! Don't let them take a mile, only an inch!

Pick a Monday to start implementing your new plan.
Bell rings!!! DON'T let anyone into the classroom! Have
the students line up in the hallway OUTSIDE the classroom.
Make sure you've got a well-behaved SLOW WALKER at the
front of the line. Quieting the kids down as much as possible. With a smiling face and a cheerful voice, "GOOD MORNING, boys and girls!! I missed you! I'm glad you're back!" In a forceful, yet controlled voice, tell the kids to walk SLOWLY to THEIR DESKS, and NOWHERE ELSE. (Winter coats and boots right to their desks with them). To your desks, please! Sally, to your desk, please! Yes, I know! But first, TO YOUR DESK, PLEASE! Thank you, Mister or Miss__________! (Smile).

Once each kid is seated, "STAY in your seats, please! NO
WANDERING AROUND! YOU MUST STAY in YOUR SEATS! always a forceful CONTROLLED voice, NEVER ANGRY!) No, John! I did not give you permission to sharpen your pencil. Sit down, please! You'll have time to do that, later! Thank you, John! (SMILE, and make sure John sees you smile!)

I told him to pick out his worst behaved kid in the class. Manufacture a compliment, if necessary! I meant to tell you. Last week, on recess duty, I was watching you play soccer. Young man, you ARE GOOD!! Where did you learn that stuff? I'm glad you're in my classroom!

Your students will notice the change. Now, on Monday, your students don't know what the heck is going on but they do know they LIKE it. The FIRST day using the NEW you is super important. The kids will try to REVERT to their OLD habits. YOU MUST STIFLE THEM IMMEDIATELY!!! Or this becomes an exercise in futility!

THE FOUNTAIN FOCUS:
WHATEVER WORKS!

FOR JUST MONDAY and the first few days next week, FORGET the timetable! FORGET the curriculum! Choose YOUR favorite topics in your FAVORITE school subjects, but not art or other noise inducing subjects. It's ABSOLUTELY IMPERATIVE that you make THIS lesson the FIRST lesson you teach on MONDAY morning.

If it's noisy (even slightly), use the hand signal!!!!! DO NOT START THE LESSON UNTIL YOU HAVE 100% ATTENTIVENESS!!

TELL, not ask, TELL the students to clear their desk tops—no pencils, no rulers, no erasers, no books, no paper, etc. NO NOTHING! You've got to get rid of the "toys". The ONLY things on the desktops are clasped hands and 2 elbows. That's crucial! Don't start your FIRST lesson until EVERY student complies. You're using peer pressure in reverse. The "usually bad behavior" kids feel obliged to comply because, now, most of their peers are complying. If some kids "unclasp" their hands, clasp your hands and STAND RIGHT in FRONT of them. I told him not to say a word. Just SMILE! and show them YOUR clasped hands!

Once you have 100% attentiveness, start your lesson! Make it a BANG UP lesson!!! The students must become CONVINCED that when our teacher talks, and if WE listen, then WE LEARN!!!!

During the instructional part of the lesson, if a kid turns around to whisper or whatever, (STOP TALKING), and announce most officiously, "I will not continue the lesson until we have FULL ATTENTION! You have no right to interfere with my lesson." (Do Not SMILE, but make a FROWN right at the student.) Soon, the students realize that the competent teacher in front of them means business! Stop talking EVERY time there's even the slightest variance from paying attention by any student. Don't say a word. Just stare and frown slightly.

When you finish up the instructional part, it's time for seatwork related to the lesson. This is a crucial time! While the seatwork is being distributed, there is a tendency for friendly chatting to start up. STIFLE it IMMEDIATELY! No noise, please! Thank you! I'm sorry, boys and girls, no one said to take out your pencils, yet! PUT them away, please. Thank you! Once every student has the seatwork on his or her desk, TELL them to take out their pencils, rulers, and erasers. (even if it's 5 seconds AFTER you told them to put them back in their desks). Yes, John! NOW, you may sharpen your pencil! NO, Tyler, wait until John has finished. Then, YOU may leave your seat to go sharpen your pencil. (SMILE) but, Tyler, not until then!! O.K., big guy! ("Handsome Dude" works wonders)

CIRCULATE! REMEDIATE! and PAY COMPLIMENTS (tons of them every day and you don't even have to smile each time you pay a compliment). Don't miss a kid! Catch each kid with a compliment at least once sometime during the day. I did this at all of my schools and it works with any grade level! Crucial!!! If you overlook a kid, nail him the first thing the next morning. "Denise, I like your jacket! Nice color. Warm, I bet?"

Nick, remember to dot your "i's". Hey, nice "p's"! Kelly, remember your loops in "e". See that "e". Make the others just like that one. Hey, Miguel! You remembered to cross your "t's". I'm so proud of you, young man! In fact, boys and girls please put your pencils down. (Wait until everyone has complied). I'm so happy with you guys and gals! Did you know that all of you are better printers than I was when I was in grade 3? O.K. crew, back to work! Anthony! You're getting better every day! How's your mom? Is she home from the hospital, yet?

I told my ACP teacher to stay in this mode for at least a couple of weeks! You will have gained TOTAL control of the classroom, gained the kids' confidence in their teacher, let the kids know in no uncertain terms that you will not tolerate any more nonsense, raised their self esteem with your positive criticisms, and convinced the students that, "Hey, school is not that bad! I really like my teacher! He makes us behave!"

When you have created a happy, caring, positive learning environment, you can get back to "group" work! But, always be ready to revert back to being a "kind leader" for as long as it takes!

Just remember, something has called on you to make the decision to teach! Hang in there! Teaching CAN be a most wonderful human experience!

My Favorite Teacher Saying:

Teach Your Students How To Think, Not What To Think!!

Chapter 33

WHAT IS THE SOLUTION FOR THE TEACHER SHORTAGE?

Maria M. says that she never thought of becoming a teacher in her country, she studied to be a doctor. "I was not going to be a teacher under any circumstances," she recalls. "But, I think I was born with certain talents." In May, Maria will be certified as a teacher. The route she took to the front of the classroom, however, is different from the traditional four-year college program. She will be one of the unique graduates of the North Harris College Teacher Certification and Education Program – part of the North Harris Montgomery College District.

This one and a half year long program prepared her well for the classroom, says Maria. "They taught us a great deal about classroom discipline, child development, child psychology, lesson cycles, instructional technology, strategies for teaching, and how to encourage children to learn. They also taught us how to work with foreign students – and the cultural shock they might go through when they come here – and how to help them."

She took the required 108 contact hours in Pedagogy and Professional Responsibilities course, received eight Saturday Seminars of additional instruction by the TCEP staff, and worked closely with a campus mentor and a North Harris College TCEP (Content-Area) Supervisor throughout the internship.

"You almost feel like a fish in a fishbowl," Maria says. "You are watched and scrutinized. You are taken aside and told how you could do it better. My school mentor and my supervisor from North Harris College TCEP took charge of me. They observed me regularly and gave me tips and pointers."

Her story is a familiar one to others who have completed alternative certification programs. Supporters of these programs say they are a "win-win" for school districts scrambling for teachers and for adults interested in pursuing a more meaningful career.

Faced with severe teacher shortages, states, including Texas, are looking at new ways to certify teachers. Alternative certification programs were introduced in the 1980's as a short-term solution to the problem but are fast becoming a permanent fix. In the past, colleges and universities took the lead on teacher certification. Now, they are competing with alternative programs administered by state education agencies and local school districts.

Why the shortfall? Fewer traditional college students are enrolling in education courses, while more veteran teachers are retiring from the field. Newer instructors are leaving only after three to five years.

"We are producing at least 330 fully qualified teachers per year and getting ready to triple this upcoming year," says Debra Fountain, program manager of the North Harris College Teacher Certification and Education Program. Those who go the traditional route to educational career and do pursue a teaching position when they graduate are less likely to teach in the challenging inner-city areas that are in desperate need of qualified teachers. The perceived crime and violence in urban areas is a real turn off, particularly to people going into their first year of teaching.

In an effort to recruit more teachers, Texas, along with along other states, are making their alternative certification programs more attractive by placing heavier emphasis on mentoring, content-area supervising, hands-on learning in the classroom, flexibility in course scheduling, and requirements for the candidates. Some argue that these approaches and other improvements have helped strengthen alternative certification programs throughout the United States.

Supporters say that alternative certification programs provide a fast track for mid-career professionals and retirees who may be less inclined to return to college and pursue a traditional education degree. Advocates say alternative certification programs offer school districts more flexibility to recruit and hire teachers, especially in urban districts with large minority populations that have been hardest hit by the teacher shortage.

New Jersey was the first state to approve alternative routes to teaching in 1985; Texas followed when the legislature authorized a similar program in the same year. Once prospective teachers are enrolled in one of the Texas's alternative certification programs, they typically begin teaching within a few months and are paid during their internship. More than 35,000 teachers have been certified through the state's alternative certification programs, many of which are affiliated with the state's community college systems. Although the programs slightly vary, all prospective teacher candidates are required to pass the same certification exams as are students enrolled in more traditional four-year university programs.

"We did an analysis of our last two cohorts, and 41% percent of people in our alternative certification program are 35 years or older," Fountain says. "We are talking about true career changers here, not merely individuals who have been unsuccessful at past careers but people who have always wanted to pursue teaching." Supporters of alternative certification echo Fountain's sentiment. They say older, more mature candidates offer a world view and are more patient – qualities, they contend, that work very well in the classroom.

Studies on how long teachers stay in the profession seem to vary as much as the alternative certification programs themselves. One study, conducted by the Texas State Board for Educator Certification, shows that nontraditionally licensed teachers stay in the profession for about as long as traditionally licensed teachers – six years. Early data from the National Center of Education Information indicate that individuals entering teaching through alternative certification routes show a higher retention rate than those graduating from traditional programs.

One of the main issues for supporters and detractors alike is, how good is good enough. The North Harris College Alternative Teacher Certification Program supporters contend that if a prospective candidate has strong content expertise in math, science, special education or bilingual education, the teaching – with proper training and mentoring – will quickly come.

State education agencies and district leaders say their backs up against the wall. When schools fail to recruit new teachers, districts must hire uncertified teachers, assign teachers out-of-field, and increase class sizes. "In the past I had to hire long-term substitute teachers," says Fountain. "I would rather hire someone who is interested in teaching as a profession and meets the qualifications for the program who has had intensive support than to have a long-term substitute."

Supporters and critics agree on one thing – there is a lot more work to be done. They say states have to do a better job of collecting data on alternative certification programs and offer more guidance on what constitutes a high-quality alternative teacher education program. Fountain stated, "I have recommended a stronger investment in performance assessments for our prospective teacher candidates who are enrolled in our non-traditional program."

Fountain says, "I predict that more colleges and universities will offer alternative certification programs and many of the newer programs either are or will be housed on college campuses. I have been tracking this issue for some time and I believe that alternative certification programs are not going anywhere. Our program draws a diversity of individuals with in-depth subject matter backgrounds."

Chapter 34

YES TO YEAR-ROUND SCHOOLS

Proponents of year-round education believe the programs will better academic achievement and alleviate overcrowding in the schools. Year-round education schedules are arranged in instructional time blocks that include shorter but more periodic vacations while maintaining the same number of days in the school year. The majority of these programs are in California, Florida, and Texas. Opponents of year-round education conclude children need the ten-week summer break for more effective learning, maturation, and rest time.

However, more than 1.7 million students will remain in classes a few weeks longer and get a shorter vacation break. They attend schools with "year-round education" (YRE) programs designed to improve student achievement and ease overcrowding. Year-round education programs rearrange the school schedule into several time blocks separated by shorter and more frequent vacation breaks. In most year-round education schedules, the number of days in the school year remains the same as in traditional calendars.

Supporters claim, among other things, that year-round education reduces learning loss during the usual ten-twelve week summer hiatus. Opponents say that time off is itself part of the learning and maturing process, and that year-round education disrupts family activities. Despite the name, year-round education does not actually require pupils to attend school all year. It is, rather, a catchall term for programs that rearrange the traditional school calendar into several instructional time blocks separated by shorter and more frequent vacation breaks. In most year- round education arrangements, the number of days in the school year is the same as in the traditional calendars.

THE FOUNTAIN FOCUS:
WHATEVER WORKS!

Year-round schooling is attracting interest at a time of mounting dissatisfaction with the state of public elementary and secondary education. Studies have repeatedly shown that American high school students score well below students from other advanced countries in core academic subjects such as mathematics and history. These countries typically require longer instructional days than most American schools. Many school officials believe that to make this country competitive the school year must lengthen. The acid test for year-round schooling, supporters and opponents agree, is whether it raises the academic achievement of students exposed to it. Many would agree with public policy that additional time by itself does not assure successful learning.

Other factors enter the picture ranging from the quality of the teacher to the quality of the textbooks to the health of the student. Time factors such as length of the school year, the length of the school week, the length of the school day, the number of minutes diverted to managing the classroom, the number of minutes allotted to a particular subject, the amount of homework, the rate of pupil attendance and absenteeism, are all interrelated and cannot be considered in isolation. Notwithstanding these complexities, opinion on the academic effectiveness of year-round education tends to be sharply divided. The intersession vacation periods benefit both students and teachers. During the three-week breaks, students have a choice of school related activities. They can continue attending school for a half-day and pick up classes either for credit or for enrichment.

One of the methodological problems with many of the studies, whatever their conclusions, is the difficulty of isolating the variable of school calendar in relation to student achievement. Does participating in year-round educational programs increase student achievement? A review of the literature indicates contradictory research results.

One body of work shows no substantial variances in student achievement between traditional calendar schools the year-round schools. States that long summer vacations are damaging as pupils' previous learning decays and precious time is consumed in reviewing curriculum at the beginning of the school year.

Conversely, other researchers assert that year-round programs minimize review time as students' learning has less time to regress. Until these inconsistencies in findings can be resolved or explained, year-round education will continue to be a controversial alternative for improving scholastic achievement. Email me at my website and let me know your YRE opinions: www.debrafountain.com

Chapter 35

POSSIBLE SOLUTIONS FOR FUTURE—ACP CANDIDATES

One of my best friends from Pittsburgh says teaching runs in her family. Her mother was a teacher, as was her grandmother. But until a year ago, she was on a different career path—one that made use of her master's degree in anthropology. "I was not going to be a teacher under any circumstances," she recalls. "But I think I was born with certain talents." In September, Karen was certified as a teacher. The route she took to the front of the classroom, however, is different from the traditional four-year college program.

This yearlong program prepared her well for the classroom, says Karen. "They taught us a great deal about child development, child psychology, strategies for teaching, and how to encourage children to learn. They also taught us how to work with foreign students—and the cultural shock they might go through when they come here—and how to help them."

She took the required 15 hours of university courses in education, received four hours of additional instruction by district staff every week, and worked closely with a mentor during her first year in the classroom.

"You almost feel like a fish in a fishbowl," Karen says. "You're watched and scrutinized. You're taken aside and told how you could do it better. My mentor took charge of me. She observed me regularly and gave me valuable tips, tricks, and terrific pointers."

Karen recently completed her first year as a certified bilingual teacher. Her story is a familiar one to others who have completed alternative certification programs. Supporters of these programs say they are a win-win for districts scrambling for teachers and for adults interested in pursuing a more meaningful career.

Faced with severe teacher shortages, states are looking at new ways to certify teachers. Alternative certification programs were introduced in the 1980s as a short-term solution to the problem but are fast becoming a permanent fix. In the past, colleges and universities took the lead on teacher certification. Now, they are competing with alternative certification programs administered by state education agencies and local school districts.

According to the National Center for Education Information in Washington, D.C., public schools will need 2.2—2.7 million teachers—both veteran teachers and new teachers to fill classroom positions in the next decade. That's at least 220,000 teachers a year for the next 10 years.

Why the deficit? Fewer traditional college students are enrolling in education courses, while more veteran teachers are retiring from the field. Newer instructors are leaving after only three to five years in the classroom.

Those who do pursue a teaching position when they graduate are less likely to teach in the challenging inner city and rural areas that are in desperate need of qualified teachers.

The perceived crime and violence in inner cities is a real turn off, particularly to young people who are going into their first job.

The competition for new teachers is fierce, especially for teachers in high-demand areas such as special education, math, science, and bilingual education. In New Mexico, prospective teachers in these specialized areas are recruited heavily by school districts in Texas and other neighboring states.

In an effort to recruit more teachers, some states are making their alternative certification programs more attractive by placing heavier emphasis on mentoring, hands-on learning in the classroom, and flexibility in scheduling and requirements for candidates. Some argue that these approaches and other improvements have helped strengthen alternative certification programs.

Supporters say alternative certification programs provide a fast track for mid-career professionals and retirees who may be less inclined to return to college and pursue a traditional education degree. Advocates say alternative certification programs offer districts more flexibility to recruit and hire teachers, especially in the urban districts with large minority populations that have been hardest hit by the teacher shortage.

New Jersey was the first state to approve alternative routes to teaching in 1985; Texas followed when the legislature authorized a similar program in the same year. Once prospective teachers are enrolled in one of Texas's 35 alternative certification programs, they typically begin teaching within a few months and are paid during their internship. More than 35,000 teachers have been certified through the state's alternative certification programs. Although the programs vary, all prospective teachers are required to pass the same certification tests as are students enrolled in a more traditional four-year college or university program.

Supporters of alternative certification say older, more mature candidates offer a world view and are more patient—qualities, they contend, that work well in the classroom.

As of 2000, 41 states and the District of Columbia had approved alternative certification programs, according to the National Center for Education Information.

Some states require courses on classroom instruction, trained full-time mentors assigned to prospective teachers, and lots of support during a prospective teacher's internship in the classroom. Other, more lenient, programs offer certification based on a transcript and a resume. Still others require individuals to complete the equivalent of a traditional teacher preparation program.

One of the core issues for supporters and detractors alike is, how good is good enough. Supporters contend that if a prospective teacher has strong content expertise in math, science, or other subject areas, the teaching—with proper training and mentoring—will quickly come. Other say not so fast...learning how to teach takes time, instruction, and lots of experience.

Supporters and critics agree on one thing—there's more work ahead. They say states have to do a better job of collecting data on alternative certification programs and offer more guidance on what constitutes a high-quality alternative teacher education program.

Some observers recommend a stronger investment in performance assessments for prospective teachers who are enrolled in traditional and nontraditional programs alike.

Many more colleges and universities are offering alternative certification programs. Many of the newer programs are housed on college campuses. "Initially, they were the biggest critics because they saw it as a big threat. Being smart people, they decided not to follow the train but to get on the front end of it."

Others are less optimistic about the impact of nontraditional licensure on the teaching profession. "I believe that people are going to take the easy way out—and the cheapest way out—as the teacher shortage continues. They will be more willing to hire people with fewer credentials and less experience, and not have to pay for mentoring."

Still others take a wait-and-see approach. I think alternative certification will solve the problem temporarily and it will attract more people into the teaching profession. But, it remains to be seen how many of these candidates who went through the program stay in teaching.

Chapter 36

IS TEACHING FOR EVERYONE?

"In the end, the preference of a job is a negotiation between what the individual in a particular life stage wants with what he or she perceives as a sensible selection."

D. L. Fountain

More than five thousand youth drop out of school everyday. The achievement gaps between racial groups and economic classes continue to widen. The persistent shortage of teachers who can be effective in 140 failing urban school systems guarantees that the malediction of 7.5 million diverse children in urban poverty will continue. Traditional university based teacher education has demonstrated for over half a century that it cannot provide teachers who will be effective and who will remain in these schools for longer than brief periods.

Recruiting and preparing teachers for the real world will require teacher education programs to FOCUS on selecting mature, diverse adults who can be prepared on-the-job teachers of record with the help of mentors and with access to technological support. These teacher education programs cannot claim that the negative conditions of work in urban schools must first be improved before they can be held accountable for providing competent teachers for diverse students in poverty.

The likelihood is that these failing school systems will get even worse as they continue to do a very big injustice with the current and future generations.

Since the models for preparing effective teachers for diverse children in poverty already exist they can and should be replicated now. The discipline in this book FOCUSes on this "promise."

It is now typical for Americans to change jobs and career paths throughout their working lives. The old paradigm of school-to-work in which individuals were trained for one job or career which they then pursued for a lifetime is long gone. The new paradigm is an iteration of school-to-work-to-school-to-work-to-school-to-work as people require constant retraining for new roles and careers.

While much has been written about this new pattern of individuals moving through many jobs and roles over a lifetime, the emphasis of this literature is top-down and external: it deals with how economic forces demand that individuals retool themselves for the global information age. While these demands are real and accelerating, the fact is that adults also respond to internal needs as they move through the stages of adult development. What a 22-year old thinks is a satisfying job, reflects a different set of needs and expectations than what a 38 or 54 year old regards as a satisfying job. In spite of denigrating terms such as "job hoppers," "retread," or "career switchers," mature individuals seeking new roles and careers in teaching is a predictable, natural, desirable response to maturation and development.

It is a healthy reaction! Those who are comfortable in precisely the same jobs at age 60 that they at age 20 are fixated in a pattern on non-growth. While American society is clearly the most flexible in allowing and supporting shifts in life choices, there are reasonable limits as well as unfortunate rigidities controlling the options open to people.

People are driven to search for the meaning at all life stages, but what seems meaningful to them changes strikingly in succeeding stages of maturity. Even in the world's most open society, the constraints and limits placed on individuals become harder to overcome as they mature and take on greater responsibilities. In the end, the choice of a job or career is a compromise between what the individual in a particular life stage wants with what s/he perceives as a realistic option.

Many who have analyzed the young adult stage of life characterize it as the age of "me-time" in which the FOCUS is on self. In contrast, middle adulthood can be characterized as a time when many desire to put meaning in their lives by helping others find their meaning in theirs. As adults shift from a FOCUS on self to more social concerns, they are motivated to reconsider their job and life opportunities. Many careers provide opportunities for helping others but require long periods of extensive preparation.

Other jobs offer the opportunity to serve others after relatively brief periods of training. Many adults ask themselves, "What should I do to put more meaning in my life without making my family suffer from becoming a student again with no income or health insurance?" The answer to this question, for many, is becoming an alternatively certified teacher through a program of paid, insured, on-the-job training in the classroom.

ATTRIBUTES OF ALTERNATIVE CERTIFICATION TEACHERS FOR URBAN SCHOOLS

While the search for meaning is the primary attraction of teaching to mature adults, there is a set of background factors that are predictive of what kind of people will be effective and remain in schools serving diverse students in poverty. Many who can become effective teachers will not have all of these attributes but the populations of mature adults who become effective and remain in these classrooms tend to have many of the following characteristics. They:

- Live in or were raised in a metropolitan area.
- Attended schools in a metropolitan area as a child or youth.
- Have had life experiences that involved extensive relationships with children.
- African American, Latino, members of a minority group, or from a working class white family.

- Earned a bachelor's degree; many started in a community college.
- Majored in a field other than education as undergraduates.
- Have had varied work experiences before seeking to become a teacher.
- Part of a family in which teaching is regarded as a fairly high-status career.
- Experienced a period of living in poverty or empathizes with the challenges of living in poverty.
- Had out-of-school experiences with children of diverse backgrounds.
- Had military experience but not as an officer.
- Engaged in volunteer activities with diverse children in poverty.
- Can multitask for extended periods of time. Unfortunately, many districts still recruit and hire only the traditionally educated pool applicants and not the alternatively certified. Again, all of these characteristics are not required but having a cluster of them is typical of individuals who succeed and stay in urban schools.

While teaching all remain a predominately, female career, more mature males can and should be recruited and prepared. As with females, the most powerful predictor is age; as more mature males are recruited, the number of who succeed and remain increases substantially. The males who succeeded in urban teaching need three additional attributes:

- Work in feminine institutions where procedures and human relationships with other adults are of greater importance than outcomes.
- Take directions and accept evaluations from female principals and female supervisors.

- Implement criticism not stated as direct orders but as "suggestions" or "concerns."

Clearly, teachers who remain in the profession and are effective exhibit the following attributes:

1. **Persistence** refers to the effective teacher's continuous search for what works best for individuals and classes. Part of this persistence involves problem solving and creative effort. The manifestation of this quality is that no student goes unnoticed or can stay off-task for very long. Effective teachers never give up on trying to engage every student.

2. **Protecting learners and learning** refers to making children's active involvement in productive work more important than curriculum rigidities and even school rules. Effective teachers not only recognize all the ways in which large school organizations impinge on students but find ways to make and keep learning the highest priority.

3. **Application of generalizations** refers to the teacher's ability to translate theory and research into practice. Conversely, it also refers to the teacher's ability to understand how specific behaviors support concepts and ideas about effective teaching. This dimension predicts the teacher's ability to benefit from professional development activities and grow as a professional practitioner.

4. **Approach to at-risk students** deals with the teacher's perceptions of the causes and cures for youngsters who are behind in basic skills. Effective teachers see poor teaching and rigid curricula as the major causes. They are also willing to assume personal accountability for their students' learning in spite of the fact that they cannot control all in-school and out-of-school influences on their students.

5. **Professional versus personal orientation to students** refers to whether teachers might use teaching to meet the their emotional needs rather than the students'. Quitter/failures have a different set of expectations than effective teachers on how they expect to relate to children. They find it difficult to respect and care about children who may do things they regard as despicable.

6. **Burnout—its causes and cures** predicts the likelihood that teachers will survive in an urban school bureaucracy. Those with no understanding of the causes of burnout who hold naïve expectations of working in school systems are most likely to be victims.

7. **Fallibility** refers to the teacher's willingness to admit mistakes and correct them. This dimension of teacher behavior establishes the classroom climate for how students respond to their mistakes in the process of learning.

Seven other functions also discriminate between greatness and failure in urban teaching. Following are these functions.

1. **High expectations:** The demonstrated belief that all the children can be successful if appropriately taught,

2. **Organizational ability**: The skill to plan, gather materials and set up a workable classroom.

3. **Physical/emotional stamina**: The ability to persist with commitment and enthusiasm after instances of violence, death and other crises.

4. **Teaching style**: The use of coaching rather than direction and information giving.

5. **Explanations of success**: An emphasis on student effort rather than presumed ability.

6. **Ownership**: The willingness to lead students to believe it is their classroom not the teacher's.

7. **Inclusion.** The acceptance of accountability for all the students assigned to the classroom.

Presently, more than 450 cities across America utilize the Urban Teacher Selection Interview, which includes the first seven functions outlined above. This very large, on-going sample provides the database for claiming that mature adults are three times more likely than younger candidates to demonstrate these functions.

THE FOUNTAIN FOCUS: WHATEVER WORKS!

A perspective:

Considering the working conditions teachers say they need versus those they regard as debilitating, the likelihood is far greater that the negative conditions under which teachers work are likely to worsen. What this means for securing teachers who will stay and become effective is clear. While all constituencies must do everything possible to try and improve the conditions under which urban teachers work, the students cannot be held hostage waiting for change agents who have been completely unsuccessful up to now. The need is to recruit and retain teachers who can be effective with *today's* children and youth in *today's* schools. Teacher educators should not be allowed to take the pious position that it is unfair or even immoral for beginning teachers to function in today's schools and therefore those who prepare teachers cannot be held accountable for the quality of their training programs until the urban schools are first transformed. There are real children and youth spending the only lives they will ever have being misadjusted in these schools everyday. Demanding that the schools improve *before* effective teachers can be prepared for such places will sacrifice still another generation. The most prudent course is to scale up the successful models of urban teacher education we now have and recruit, select and prepare caring effective, mature teachers who will make a difference immediately.

"If you are here in this world among us, it is because the world needs you! Do something to change the world positively!!"

Chapter 37

CLASSROOM STRUCTURE IDEAS

FOCUS ON BEHAVIOR:
Specific attitudes and actions of this child at home and/or at school. Doesn't pay attention in class. Doesn't do assignments and, therefore, has poor grades. Will not enter into any class discussions, or discussions regarding anything. Has a poor sense of self. Immature and easily distracted due to relatively unimportant matters. Has a short attention span. Frequently absent, tardy, or both. Isolates him/herself socially. Generally has a sloppy personal appearance and negative attitude. Displays "I don't care" attitude in everything that he/she does. In many ways, seems emotionally dead. Tends to be slow in physical movements—even in leaving class. Doesn't have a lot of friends. Personal history is not marked by success. May watch TV excessively, or spend time driving or riding in cars.

FOCUS ON EFFECTS:
How behavior affects teachers, classmates, and parents in the school learning environment and the home family situation. Other marginal students are influenced to become apathetic as well. Importance of academic work and the school itself is diminished. Teacher becomes frustrated easily and frequently with his/her lack of success in trying to motivate this student. Class morale is often lowered. Other students often become disturbed and can't concentrate themselves. Teacher often devotes too much time to the apathetic student, and ends up losing control of the class. Continued prodding during class time is necessary. Necessity of make-up work, extended deadlines, and varied standards is increased. Teacher may ignore student's existence if he/she is not a troublemaker.

FOCUS ON ACTIONS:
Identify causes of misbehavior. Pinpoint student needs being revealed. Employ specific methods, procedures, and techniques at school and at home for getting the child to modify or change his/her behavior. Primary cause of misbehavior: Self-Confidence: Due to a feeling that he/she has little worth, this student feels rejected. Primary needs being revealed: Escape from Pain: The apathetic person is feeling a lot of pain and chooses to be apathetic as a means of insulating him/herself from others who might possibly cause him/her pain. Secondary needs being revealed: Affiliation: This student needs to develop a close friendship with an adult or peer. Gregariousness: This student needs to belong to a group of some kind. Such a membership increases motivation. Status: He/she needs to improve self-esteem and develop a sense of being a worthwhile person, important to someone. Provide the student with short-term tasks for which goals are clearly seen and clearly achievable. This strategic action is an absolute. Ask for his/her opinions during class and after class. Give concrete rewards for any altered behavior. Find a "payoff" for the apathetic student, which will turn him/her on to learning in the school. It may be an extra-class activity. Remember, involvement is a key. Therefore, involve the student in the learning process by creating a sense of ownership. It must be the student's room, teacher, and class, before he/she will become involved. Never forget, this student doesn't believe anything belongs to him/her. Attempt to make materials more relevant and available to the student. Accept the fact that not everything that happens in the classroom or in the school is going to be of interest to everyone, and that some students who are not really apathetic may be labeled thus erroneously. Contact parents immediately when you begin to observe this problem. Don't wait until the student is so far behind in his/her work that this, rather than the apathetic behavior, becomes the primary problem. Seek input from the counselor or from other teachers who have had this student in their classes. At every opportunity, express your concern and your desire for this student to succeed. Until you can give the student a win, he/she will remain apathetic. Therefore, consider adjusting your standards to reach this student. This action is a primary consideration in changing the behavior. Too, you may have to forget make-up work.

DO NOT JUST FOCUS ON MISTAKES:
Common misjudgments and errors in managing the child which may perpetuate or intensify the problem. Failing to create opportunities for this

student to succeed. Ignoring the student altogether, or assuming he/she doesn't want to learn. Failing to check to see that the student is completing assignments on a daily basis. Requiring less from this student than we do from other students. Failing to make a sincere effort to really get to know the student personally. Confronting the student in front of the class. Assuming that the student is physically well and ready to learn

FOCUS ON BEHAVIOR II:
Specific attitudes and actions of this child at home and/or at school. May be a student who can't do well, one who has not done as well as he/she should, or one who is being passed reluctantly. Underachievement can mean different things to different teachers. Regardless, experiences failure. This is the common thread. May be scared. May not feel very good about him/herself. Susceptible to peer group pressure. Likely to be very bored. Doesn't accept responsibility. Doesn't work up to his/her abilities. Has poor study habits and usually doesn't do his/her homework assignments.

FOCUS ON EFFECTS II:
How behavior affects teachers, classmates, and parents in the school learning environment and the home family situation. Teacher is concerned and frustrated. In truth, the underachiever may be concerned too. Lessons being learned in class begin to seem unimportant to other students. Parents are upset because they believe teacher isn't teaching correctly. Other kids—especially borderline students—get pulled down to a level of underachieving with this student.

FOCUS ON ACTIONS II:
Identify causes of misbehavior. Pinpoint student needs being revealed. Employ specific methods, procedures, and techniques at school and at home for getting the child to modify or change his/her behavior. Primary cause of misbehavior: Self-Confidence: The inability to achieve causes a great deal of insecurity. Primary need being revealed: Escape from Pain: This student has experienced a great deal of failure and is very fearful of risking future academic attempts. Secondary need being revealed: Achievement: This student needs tasks that are within his/her ability range. If any student needs achievement, it is the underachiever. An especially difficult student attitude to counteract is "playing it safe." The student with this attitude won't aim high because he/she doesn't want to be disappointed. Changing this attitude

takes time. However, the only way to begin is by rewarding effort as well as achievement. Praise and encourage the student's initiative. But don't push this student, or he/she will never move out of the "safe zone." Recognize one fact, and you can do a great deal to change student attitudes: While the successful student experiences success in front of others, the underachiever usually experiences failures publicly and successes privately. That's the difference—and the problem. Recognize that this is a problem best handled by all teachers, administrators, parents, and child working together. Acknowledge the fact that this student wastes time. Recognize the four biggest time wasters: laziness, procrastination, distraction, and impatience. And know that these time-consuming mistakes are abetted by a lack of preparation, thoroughness, or perseverance. Most often, the underachiever scores low in all these areas. Call parents. Be aware that most parents come to school expecting resistance. Many think their child tried, but couldn't resolve the difficulty for a variety of reasons, none of them good. Therefore, asking parents, "What can I do?" is disarming. Likewise, you'll be amazed how parents change their tune when you say, "What can we do together?" "Together" is a great word. It means sharing. It says, "You do something, and we will too." If parents respond with a request outside the realm of your authority, say so. But also say, "Let's help." Teachers often assign additional work to underachievers. Be aware that sometimes the opposite approach produces better results. If a student won't do class assignments, don't allow him/her to participate. Insist that the student sit idly. Remember, even when kids won't do assigned work, they still want to participate with the group. Being included is very important to children. Sometimes, kids can learn a very valuable lesson, and arrive at better decisions, if they are forbidden to work for short periods of time. Some underachievers may change their values and actions more quickly if they are sometimes not permitted to work. Never use class work as punishment. Such a practice only reinforces the negative feelings the underachiever has for school. Remember, problem students already possess negative attitudes. Therefore, if you're going to punish, use a form of punishment that is not a part of the classroom learning experience, and you may solve a problem rather than compound one. Don't put the underachiever down or make him/her feel insignificant in any way. If you do, you may be inadvertently denying the prestige motivator in learning. Likewise, if you don't give recognition for success, you can't use the prestige motivator effectively. Don't frighten the underachiever or make threats concerning grades or behavior. The insecurity produced may be counterproductive to motivation and may make the problem worse. Don't be cold, sarcastic, or intolerant. The underachiever may learn the wrong lessons from such approaches. Most of all, this student needs a firm, caring, and unified effort from all the adults in his/her life. If the student does not try, withdraw privileges at school. Notify parents; they may want to take similar action at home. Be careful about telling a student he/she can't pass your course or class. You may not only lose a student's interest and motivation from now until the end of school—you may also be creating a discipline problem. Remember, when hope is gone, so is interest. Then, the stage is set for a discipline problem to develop. Writing comments on student papers such as "This isn't worth grading," or crumpling a student assignment and throwing it in the wastebasket can completely demoralize a student. Never belittle any student effort. Your challenge as a professional teacher is to motivate students to improve their efforts. Rejection only creates another teacher hurdle. Talk to this student about his/her strengths and possibilities. The underachiever already knows his/her weaknesses. Make specific recommendations for things this student can do during the summer. Research summer courses and have enrollment forms available. Give this student summer assignments and volunteer to see him/her during the summer. Even if the student does not respond, your offer has conveyed an important message. Your interest alone can give hope—and maybe motivation not to give up. Maintain contact with parents—and talk with next year's teachers as well. Remember, perspective reveals that most students will grow up to be responsible and productive adults. They need to remember our belief in them. These students can learn—if given time. Your own self-confidence can work for you rather than against you if you take the right approach with students. First, be careful about telling. Second, take extreme care not to talk in absolute terms when sharing ideas or suggestions. Even when all the evidence is in, be careful about projecting the image that what you think and say is the only way to do things. Such actions are exclusive rather than inclusive. They put people down—and maybe even out of one's life. Likewise, ask rather than demand. And when you are asking, always remember to tell why you are making the request. Telling people what to do may be the easiest, quickest way to get something done. But it's seldom the best. Offering a reason takes away the air of superiority and bossiness associated with demand. It also reduces error, because when people know why they are doing something, they are more competent in doing it. If you want self-confidence to work for you, simply try making others feel as important as they really are. Then you'll surely be important to them. Without teaching, students may never know these truths. We may not either. That's why these principles need discussion. Remember, final memories are dominant. Your final action should enable students to say that they "made it" with you rather than in spite of you.

DO NOT JUST FOCUS ON MISTAKES II:
Common misjudgments and errors in managing the child which may perpetuate or intensify the problem. Quitting on the underachiever. This is the worst thing we can do. As long as we don't quit—even if the student has—hope remains. Thinking it's too late to do anything this year. It is not. Next year offers a new beginning, which may be the result of our final influence. That's why we must not quit.

FOCUS ON BEHAVIOR III:
Specific attitudes and actions of this child at home and/or at school.
A compulsive talker. Loves to talk, and engages in the practice with one and all constantly. Talks to teachers continually. Talks to other students continually. Will even talk to him/herself. Makes irrelevant comments—at inappropriate times. A poor listener. Often does not realize that he/she is talking. When teacher corrects, says, "I wasn't talking to him; he was talking to me." Has a short attention span. Craves attention. Lacks interest and is very poorly motivated. Poorly prepared for class and seldom does class work thoroughly or carefully.

FOCUS ON EFFECTS III:
How behavior affects teachers, classmates, and parents in the school learning environment and the home family situation.
Classmates and teacher alike are annoyed. Both classroom setting and lessons are disrupted. Starting class is difficult. Everyone's attention is distracted. Others are encouraged to talk. Teacher's authority is undermined. Teacher is put on the defensive when this student claims to be "picked on." Teacher is required to reprimand continually. If classmates are encouraged to talk, they get in trouble as well. Classmates begin to believe teacher is unfair, unkind, mean, and bad tempered. Time is diverted from the rest of the class. Serious learning cannot continue for any length of time.

FOCUS ON ACTIONS III:

Identify causes of misbehavior.
Pinpoint student needs being revealed.
Employ specific methods, procedures, and techniques at school and at home for getting the child to modify or change his/her behavior.
Primary cause of misbehavior:
Attention: The continual talking is a way to get attention. Primary need being revealed: Sexuality: This person has a strong social need. Personal interaction is very important.
Secondary needs being revealed:
Affiliation: This student needs to develop a close association with a peer or adult. Aggression: This student is attempting to become positively involved with the class or teacher and does not realize that he/she is expressing a negative behavior.
Achievement: This student needs to experience some kind of success through talking, but without disrupting the class and the teacher.
Status: This person needs to have others know that he/she is "somebody."

Remember, this is more a social problem than a discipline problem. If treated as a discipline problem, it may become one. The ability to talk is not a negative—nor is it a liability. It's an asset, which the student must learn to manage for personal benefit. Be aware that this is often a compulsive behavior. It lies between assertion and aggression in a person with a low self-concept. Never assume the student knows he/she is talking: The student may or may not know. Never assume classmates know the student is talking: They might not even hear. Remember, your relationship with one student affects your relationship with all students. How you handle this student can damage your relationship with other students. Don't show a side of you that you don't want other students to see.
First, react consistently—and never punish irrationally. Don't "get on" the talker one day, and ignore him/her the next. Equally important, don't criticize publicly. You will never solve this problem during class time. Private counseling is a must. Approach talking as a social problem, not a discipline problem. This is a counseling situation that requires a plan to change behavior. Look for the reason for the talking. If you cannot or will not meet the student's needs, you will not change the behavior. The talker has a strong activity need. Give this student small tasks and responsibilities daily to fulfill this need. Tell the student you will call on him/her during class discussion. You may even tell the student the question you will be asking.

Seat the talker near quiet and serious students.

Station yourself next to this student's desk during presentations. This will keep him/her from talking. When this student is talking, don't stop class or say a word. Rather, walk toward his/her desk. This will stop the talker. Likewise, look at this student often.

Develop a set of hand signals to remind the student when he/she is talking. Don't stop class and reprimand, however.

Capture and hold attention by calling on the talker often.

Challenge this student. Never forget, the articulate are often high achievers. The talker should be a good student. Reinforce positive behavior and contributions in class.

Provide alternate materials that can interest this student and that are still class oriented. Try incentive programs to encourage attention and preparation.

To encourage the talker to participate positively, allow him/her to take roll, pass out papers, etc.

In a private conference, tell the student,

"The ability to speak is your asset. Therefore, use it wisely by following some tips.

First, think before you speak so that you gain a reputation for being a thinker rather than a talker.

Second, speak slowly so that people can absorb what you say.

Third, speak quietly and gently to gain the reputation of being a person of depth.

Finally, limit your talking.

Remember, you can always add a comment, but you can't withdraw one."

Discuss the behavior with parents. Find time to listen.

DO NOT JUST FOCUS ON MISTAKES III:

Common misjudgments and errors in managing the child, which may perpetuate or intensify the problem.

Showing anger and frustration. This does nothing to help the situation. In fact, it may make the talker anxious and nervous—and cause him/her to talk even more.

Saying things like "Shut up" (there are over 100 polite ways to say be quiet in class…)

Interrupting class to reprimand.Attempting to belittle or shame the talker, or being sarcastic.

Punishing the entire class or creating peer pressure.

Making rules and regulations for the entire class because of this one student. Assuming classmates are disturbed by the talker—or acting on such an assumption. Classmates might not even hear.
Reacting inconsistently—and punishing irrationally.
*Overreacting by immediately rearranging the seating chart or issuing threats or ultimatums. *Isolating this student. The talker's need for attention or security will not allow his/her personality to take isolation.
*Becoming so frustrated that we say and do things we'll wish we hadn't.
*Failing to look for reasons behind the constant talking.
*Assuming the talking is directed against us personally or against class work, or that the student is uninterested, or that the talking is intended to be disrespectful.
*Assuming there is a short-term solution.
*Allowing talkers to visit after finishing lessons for the day.
*Restricting the talker to the point at which he/she isn't making a contribution at any time. *Trying to humiliate the talker, calling attention to the behavior, or trying to get the student to be quiet by placing emphasis on the behavior.

Chapter 38

FOCUSING ON POSITIVE FRAMEWORK

Discipline seems to be what you use (or desire), when student behavior is interfering with the operations in the classroom. In a sense, negative student behavior of this type gives us a clear indication that our classroom management is proving inadequate.

We see classroom management as the positive framework we lay down in the effort to promote student behavior that is conducive to the learning goals of the class. Our concerns with discipline as such mean that we are in search of an effective mending process.

Naturally the subject of student motivation is subtly entwined with both discipline and classroom management. To a great extent these three must be taken into account. FOCUSing on any one of these areas in search of an answer to a problem is quite likely to be looking at just one facet of the solution.

A terrific strategy that has worked well for me, if I have to speak to a student privately about his/her behavior, is to ask questions rather than lecture. For example, "What do you think I'm going to say to you?" "Why do you think you are here?" "What kind of behavior do you think will assist you in getting the most out of this class?" And so on…I find that if I can elicit from the student what the problem is, he/she is more likely to pay attention to this "attitude adjustment". I usually end it with saying, "What can I expect from you from now on?" The usual response becomes an informal contract and allows me to remind them of it in a very brief, but nevertheless effective, way in any future repetition of such behavior.

TIPS AND TIDBITS:

Dear D. L.

Hello all. I am teaching 7 and 8 in Spanish. Since they need to learn in a more relaxed environment that encourages language expression and experimentation…how do I achieve that and still maintain order and control in the class?

Many times, as they are truly having fun and trying out new expressions they get loud, talk about other things, and just cut up. My call to stay on task isn't always heeded. Is it this age group? Are there any songs or short sayings we can do as a sign to come back down to planet earth? Any exercises? All suggestions would be most appreciated. Thank you.

D. L. -

IDEA #1—Give them short time limits—you may even want to use a stopwatch. "We are going to do this for 3 minutes. Go!" Then stop them and have them be completely quiet. At first, you will be mainly training them to "Stop" and "Go". They will be geared, and so will not be able to maintain "completely quiet" for very long. Sequencing is important. Wildest stuff just before the bell rings to send them somewhere else. But the very last thing I want to hear in my classroom is the humming of the fluorescent lights, which tells me that I have completely lost control because they are asleep or brain-dead. Might as well teach rocks to swim.

IDEA #2—I learned this trick in a cooperative learning workshop: When students are doing a speaking activity and you want to stop the activity and get their attention, raise your hand. Teach them to do 3 things when they see your hand raised. 1) stop talking immediately, 2) SILENTLY signal their partners to stop talking (without touching, shoving, hitting, etc.), and 3) raise their hand. You have stopped the activity without trying to yell over their voices. It also helps to give them a time limit—it keeps them on task. Hope it helps—it works with high school age students too.

IDEA # 3—Here's one idea from past years at the middle school. This may seem to reach back to elementary school, but if it works for you it could help. Teach the kids that when it is time to come back together you will give them a countdown and everyone will need to join in. You will put one hand in the air and call out the numbers from five to zero backwards in the target language (counting off by show of fingers). Students are to join in with you as soon as they catch on. At 'zero' there should be complete silence. Any student still talking could be required to do something (serious or light-hearted, you decide).

IDEA # 4—If you really need to "call roll", make it an active, productive thing students must respond promptly with something at the tips of their tongues. This can be around a particular topic to review vocabulary, such as items of clothing or food; making it a rule that none can be repeated forces them to listen to those going before; requiring the article and giving an extra check/point to anyone who corrects a previous error also makes them listen.

IDEA # 5—This may be old-fashioned, but a seating chart prepared by the teacher still works! It breaks up the little cliques of friends who cluster together and want to chat. Intermingling carefully the boys and the girls also helps. It also means that you probably don't have to call roll, since an empty seat tells you immediately.

IDEA # 6—Over plan, with a variety of activities. Students who are busy doing productive work don't have the inclination (or at least the time) to act out.

IDEA # 7—At least the first time, make clear what the purpose of each activity is, so that they know how it will benefit them and support their learning. Otherwise they see some activities as just "busy work" and don't take them seriously.

IDEA # 8—Have an immediate activity ready to start class. If it's a particularly rambunctious class, make it a written activity for a clearly limited time, so that they have to get to it and get it done. Each class has its own personality—some need calming down at the beginning, some toward the end as they get tired. (And some, always!)

IDEA # 9—Always have on hand some kind of extra quiet activity that you can turn to in an emergency—when you have to take some student out in the hall to talk to them, or when your head is exploding and you just can't take any more!

IDEA # 10—If you have planned an activity that requires something in the way of technology—even as simple as the overhead projector or reserving the computer lab. Try to have on hand a backup in case of tech failure: an extra bulb; the same material on the board or on a poster, etc.

IDEA # 11—This is a private choice, but I generally don't want information about the behavior of any student from a previous teacher, as it subtly changes my attitude toward that student from the beginning and can becoming a self-fulfilling prophecy.

IDEA # 12—Imagine that your students want to learn and that they will behave. (It may sound strange to state that, but I've known teachers to go into new classes with the opposite attitude and invite misbehavior.) Have few rules, state them clearly, and enforce them kindly but firmly, with clearly stated consequences. NEVER threaten, and even more so, not with threats you probably can't enforce. [My Favorite Saying Is That Positive Reinforcement Is The Key!]

IDEA # 13—NEVER get into an exchange with a difficult student in front of the class! An audience is what they often crave. Take them out into the hall if you absolutely have to resolve the issue, or insist that they come by after school or whenever.

IDEA # 14—Related to that, don't feel you have to justify absolutely everything—you are the adult and the professional in charge of that room, and some things just ARE! There will often be the (usually very intelligent but wacky) student who loves to match wits with you, and a lot of the class time can be wasted in empty argument.

IDEA # 15—If you should have one or more real troublemakers, one strategy that has worked for me is to arrange with nearby teacher that period to send the offender(s) to them with written work to do. You've removed their known audience; put them in an unfamiliar environment. You've kept the problem within the department, rather than turning to what may be your last resort—the administration—something you don't want to do lightly.

IDEA # 16—If you've planned carefully, don't let yourself get distracted and off the track by unrelated questions designed to do just that—unless, of course, you see here an opportunity to do so in a topic of genuine interest to all.

IDEA # 17—Planning carefully doesn't mean that you don't pick up on spontaneous leads that present themselves as a good learning opportunity ignoring a comment or a question that, although not on the topic at hand, is clearly an avenue of interest and practice in the sends the message that this language isn't really meant for meaningful communication.

IDEA # 18—Be very careful about personal jokes and humor, unless you know your students extremely well—feelings are easily hurt at this age, and an innocent joke that is felt to be at someone's expense can cause trouble.

IDEA # 19—Move around the room—don't teach sitting behind your desk, or always standing in front. This not only changes the focal point, but allows students to continually move around a bit in their chairs even when the activity isn't physical—and that releases some extra energy. It also allows you to see better who's trying to do their homework in
class, etc.!

IDEA #20—Physical proximity to a student is also a controlling factor. I'm not talking about a threatening type posture—just that it's generally easier for someone to act out from a distance.

IDEA # 21—There used to be a saying "Don't smile until January!" That's obviously an exaggeration—but it is true that it is better to start out somewhat strict—you can always loosen up, whereas it's often very hard to tighten up. All of us often have our "favorite" classes—but I've found in the past that my favorites at the end of the year are often not the same ones, and sometimes I've been the cause of the change by not holding the line with some.

IDEA # 22—Avoid empty praise. In these days of the emphasis on "self-esteem" it is easy to fall into the trap of constant praise for very little. Students aren't fools, and they know when it's empty. True self-esteem is raised when the praise is unmistakably deserved, and when it isn't just given for everything.

IDEA # 23—Finally, remember why you're here—because you love your subject and think it's important, and because you like kids! If you present a decently organized class and let those two qualities shine through, you probably won't have to worry about any of the above!

IDEA # 24—On the high school or junior high side, a good classroom management trick to eliminate an unwanted behavior: After the student has committed the behavior and has not ceased after being spoken to one-on-one, in class, indirectly, directly, and any other way possible, I would ask the student to stay with me after school. When the student arrives, I gave a sheet with three questions:

1. What behavior did you demonstrate in the classroom, which caused you to have detention here with me?
2. Why is this behavior unacceptable in this classroom?
3. What is your plan to improve your behavior? How can I help you to improve your behavior?

After the student has answered the three questions, and we have discussed each in detail, then I informed the student that I would keep the writing on file for the remainder of the school year. If the problem persists, then we will call a conference with the student, student's parents, and myself to review the plan and make modifications to the plan.

Incredible—I've only had to have one conference with parents!

IDEA # 23—For everything else—I have found that humor is the key. Say it with a smile, empathize, and emphasize the fact that the student made a choice—you are not inflicting the punishment: I know how frustrating it is when one forgets things, but I'll bet you'll remember next time. I'm sorry that you chose to socialize instead of visiting the restroom, but I know that you can make it and that you'll remember to take care of your business first next time.

IDEA # 24—As to misbehavior—give the student a choice: You can either work quietly or sit here with me/in the hall. You can either stop punching Austin or you can spend lunchtime with me. Make sure that you've thought through possible consequences in advance so that the choice you offer is one you can live with. Generate a list of possible consequences in your mind so that when a situation occurs, you are not caught off guard—you know exactly how you will handle it. Obviously, you have to "read" the situation and be somewhat flexible. However, just having a bag of tricks from which you can draw will make things much easier.

IDEA # 25—As to cheating—Before the first test or quiz, I would post a list of test-taking rules and go through them as though I were an airline flight attendant.

> -Please face forward at all times.
> -Keep your eyes on your own paper at all times. No talking or lip moving.
> -You may not use books, notes, dictionaries, or electronic devices.-No cheating.
> -Remain seated and quiet until I call for the tests.

Then, I tell them that if they break one of the rules (on purpose or inadvertently) during testing time, I will walk quietly to their desk, pick up their test booklet and answer sheet, and that they will not be allowed to finish the exam. I emphasize that this does not mean that I am accusing them of cheating, but simply that I saw them break one of the test-taking rules. I explain that they will receive a zero and that the subject will not be open for discussion.

The remarkable thing about this is that I RARELY had confrontations with students-ALMOST NEVER. (When I did, I would simply tell them that I would more than happy to discuss it with them after class or during Saturday Seminar). I guess it goes back to the old idea that if you say something to them, everything just escalates. By walking over and picking up the paper silently, I am putting them in the position of having to make the first move (which would call even MORE attention to them) so most choose not to do so. When I returned to my desk, I would mark a zero on the paper and write a brief explanation of the reason—not just cheating, but an explanation of how (book open on the floor, looked at Tina's paper (and list the times I observed it), used a cheat sheet (which I staple to the test). That way, if a parent confronts me about a grade, I have the explanation right there. Document, document, and document!!!

Above all else—BE CONSISTENT and FOLLOW THROUGH. If you threaten or promise it, be sure that you act on it. Don't be afraid to say no and don't worry about trying to get the students to like you. They need to respect you first!

IDEA # 26—Do you know enough about your students' parents to have a sense of the kind of support you might expect from them? If so, I'd suggest a call home following this type of scenario:

1. Seek the aid of your disciplinary administrator by asking him/her to sit in on the phone call home.
2. During a time that you can access the student(s) have him/her/them report to you in the administrator's office.
3. Explain to the student that you are not happy with his/her behavior.
4. Hand him/her the phone and ask him/her to call one of his/her parents
to explain why his/her French teacher would like to speak with the parent.
5. Once his/her explanation is given speak with the parent
indicating specifics of the inappropriate behavior.

IDEA # 27—A couple of things that have helped me greatly over two decades:

1. Have an explicit discipline plan and post it in the classroom.
2. Follow the plan.

#2 sounds easy, but I find that a lot of teachers have trouble with it. If your plan says that you'll send a negative letter home when Joseph swings from the ceiling, send the letter. If the plan says that you'll call Crystal's mom and tell her what a wonderful child she reared because Crystal's conduct grade stayed on A all week, call her. If the plan says that it's time for Anthony to go to the office, send him. Send him with no expectations. It's out of your hands. Let the administration handle it.

IDEA # 28—Here are a few ideas for those Constant Conversationalists:

1. Walk and stand by one of the offending parties.
2. Stop talking. Make significant eye contact. Do not begin again until it is absolutely silent.
3. Never try to shout over student noise with directions or content.
4. Firmly tell students the expectation that, "When I'm talking, you are not. I am not able or willing to shout above noise." You can appeal to their sense of fairness, too. "Excuse me, but there's 30 of you and one of me." This can be a follow up to #2 if you feel it necessary.
5. Do not repeat directions a gazillion times. Do not answer questions from students who were talking while you were explaining an activity. Let them "stew in their juices." There must be consequences for not listening when you are talking.
6. I have some students who feel that they are an exception to all rules and expectations. Sometimes I have to break it to them that, "Nothing you could possibly be saying is more important than what I am saying right now." This is real "toughlove". Obviously, use with discretion.

IDEA # 29—School kids are a real work in progress, and will have bad days—but they want to grow up, so it helps to treat them as if they are—as much as possible. Try to enjoy them. Be interested in their lives out of school. Let them know you saw their name in the paper, or congratulate them on their play in the game. Change activities often. Be over-prepared. Try to do some active things to get them out of their seats at least once every day or two. Try activities that let non-academic kids shine: art projects, music . . . I've had kids make paper puppets and then use them to put on a skit. Some of the puppets were very creative. Middle school kids are a challenge—but they really can be fun. Hang in there!

IDEA # 30—An article in the London Times tells us that Mozart may soothe the savage breast. After one of my science teachers, who found herself having to deal with an almost uncontrollable class, a group of 13 slow learners, ten of whom had been identified as having emotional behavior problems, took to playing concertos by the maestro, noise levels dropped and the quality of work improved to such an extent that most were only one level behind expectations for 14 year-olds when they took national curriculum tests. My science teacher still believes until this day that Mozart works because he wrote in a higher register than other composers. Also, academics at London University found that hyperactive children benefited most from the calming influence of music played during math lessons—but pupils of all types increased their work-rate.

IDEA # 31—I have utilized a "consequence" that works WONDERFULLY in my classes. When I have a student who makes a major disruption in my class, they are required to come after school and behave. When they ask what that means, I explain to them that I expect them to be in my room at 2:50 and I will explain it to them then. When they arrive (after I call home to make sure they can stay) I have them sit in their assigned seat and behave for 30 minutes. That means that they just sit in their seat. They are not allowed to do anything else other than sit in their seat and behave. They can't read, sleep, talk, grunt, write…nothing. They just sit there. Any time they make a disturbance during the 30-minute period, their time begins all over again. I have yet to have a repeat offender. They HATE sitting there, and it really isn't a problem for me because I grade papers, straighten my room, etc. all while they are behaving. In the 30 minutes they sit in their seats, they learn a valuable lesson: "It is more fun to behave during class with me than it is to come in and behave after-school. I am not mean about this; I am very matter-of-fact about it. The students know what I expect and when they break my rules, they expect a consequence. Peer pressure really works with classroom consequences too!

Chapter 39

MAKING YOUR NEW SCHOOL YEAR NOTE-WORTHY!

Life is originality and discovery. From the flash of birth we are exposed to a steady flow of sensory experience—sight, sound, smell, taste and touch. Our incredible brain takes the images and sounds, the feelings, scents and tastes of each moment to create an inner diagram of the peripheral planet. In the establishment of life, all is new. Each occurrence is a first. Each representation, melody, scent, and embrace bathes the newborn's brain as it attempts to arrange and make sense of this world. Over time, we form memories, and we learn.

And it is in the wisdom from first experiences that our expectations are directed—the first grin, the first expressions, the first hug, the first devotion, the first defeat, and the first days of school. These unmarked experiences outline our emotions, values, principles, and behaviors. Our first experiences generate the podium from which we will analyze the rest of our life.

Over time, there are fewer firsts—the world becomes more memorable, less fresh. For many, vigorous learning slows in age. For those who find delight in discovery, however, there will be a period of wisdom. They will seek novelty and reap the rewards of mastering new experiences—maturity, creativity and wisdom. We wish this gift for our children.

Every September, thousands of young children enter a classroom for the first time and swim in innovation. Indeed, for these children, the first days of school are filled with more new experiences than any other time aside from birth. There will be new sights, sounds, schedules; new children, adults, challenges, and expectations. How can we help our children find enjoyment in these first classroom experiences that will lead to a lifelong appetite for knowledge? The key is protection.

Optimal education is a driven by inquisitiveness, which leads to exploration, discovery, practice, and mastery. In turn, mastery leads to pleasure, satisfaction, and confidence to once again explore. The more a child experiences this cycle of wonder, the more she can create a lifelong excitement and love of learning. The cycle of wonder, however, can be stopped by fear.

The apprehension response is deeply ingrained in the human brain. Under threat of any kind—hunger, thirst, pain, shame, confusion, or too much, too new or too fast—we respond in ways to keep us safe. Our minds will FOCUS only on the information that is, at that moment, important for survival. Fear kills curiosity and inhibits exploration.

This is important for the first days of school because the brain tends to interpret novelty as threatening. In new and strange settings, a young child will be overwhelmed by more novelty and find little pleasure in "learning."

Fortunately, there is another deeply ingrained feature of the human brain—curiosity. We are fascinated by and drawn to the mysterious—to new things. Humans are explorers. When we are safe and the world around us is familiar, we crave novelty. When a child feels safe, curiosity lives. Yet when the world around us is strange and new, we crave familiarity. In new situations a child will be more easily overwhelmed, distressed, and frustrated. This child will be less capable of learning. The hungry child, the ill, tired, confused, or fearful child does not care about new things—they want familiar, comforting, and safe things.

In the first weeks of school, very young children are almost drowning in novelty. We can make these new experiences easier. We can do things to make the environment more predictable, structured, familiar, and, thereby, safe. It is the invisible yet powerful web of relationships in the classroom that creates an optimal learning environment. The most important learning "tool" is the teacher. And it is the teacher who creates the safe "home base" from which the child will explore.

A sense of safety comes from consistent, attentive, nurturing, and sensitive attention to each child's needs. Safety is created by predictability, and predictability is created by consistent behaviors. And the consistency that leads to predictability does not come from rigidity in the timing of activities it comes from the consistency of interaction from the teacher. If a schedule is consistent, but the teacher is not, there is no predictability for the child. Predictability in time means less to a young child than predictability in people.

How can a teacher provide this? Use your most powerful teaching tool, your personality. Your smile, your voice, and your touch make a child feel safe. Face-to-face, "on the floor time," and eye contact are essential in this process. Be predictable in your interactions with the child and not in the number of minutes spent in each activity. Be attuned to each child's overload point. Let children find some space and solitude when they seem to be overwhelmed. In these quiet moments the child can find pleasure in reviewing the discoveries of the day.

Chapter 40

SCHOOL AND CLASS PLEDGES

I am somebody.
The me I see is the me I'll be.
I can be respectful, responsible and resourceful.
I can succeed.

I am in school to learn.
I will follow the directions of my teachers.
I will not say unkind things to others.
I will report problems to the teachers.
I will try my very best.
I am in school to learn.

I make mistakes so I can learn.
I learn so I can succeed.
I succeed so I can help others.

I pledge to show my respect
by listening to others,
using my hands for helping,
caring about others feelings,
and being responsible for what I say and do.

I am wonderful.
I am good at learning.
And I like to learn.

Chapter 41

STOP BLAMING THE TEACHER!

Last year, I was presenting a "6 Thinking Hats" workshop to my ACP candidates in the North Harris College Alternative Certification Program located in Houston, Texas. Afterwards, I was discussing educational topics with the entire group in the auditorium. Some of the secondary teachers were asking me questions about grading, motivational strategies, classroom discipline techniques that work and do not work, and their students in general…etc. They stated that the same familiar pattern leapt out at them each time they had to average their 9 weeks grades.

The students who had emigrated from foreign countries often aced every test, while many of the United States born students from upper class homes with educated parents were happy with D's and C's.

As one would expect, the middle-class American students usually had higher Language Arts grades than did their immigrant classmates, many of whom had only been speaking English for a few years.

Many of the American students that my teachers taught did not have the motivation, self-discipline or work ethic of the foreign-born kids.

Politicians can talk until their blue in the face about reform, but until the work ethic of American students change, little will happen.

Studies released a decade ago suggest that the reason so many U.S. students are "falling short of their intellectual potential" is not "inadequate teachers, boring textbooks and large class sizes" and the rest of the usual reasons cited by the so-called reformers—but "their failure to exercise self-discipline."

The disheartening fact is that in the United States, hard work on the part of students is no longer seen as a major factor in academic success. When asked to identify the most important factors in the performance in math, the percentage of Japanese and Taiwanese students who answered, "studying hard" was twice that of American students. American students named native intelligence, and some said the home environment. But a clear majority of U.S. students put the responsibility on their teachers. A good instructor was the determining factor in how well they did in math.

While I was growing up and being educated in Pittsburgh, Pennsylvania, parents didn't listen when kids complained about the teachers. Today, the teachers are supposed to miraculously make their students learn and FOCUS even though they are not working. Teachers can only do so much…when you do not have parental involvement.

Since I graduated from Duquesne University and began teaching, I have seen this trend developing over the last 20 years. It's the students who have the power. When they don't do the work and get lower grades, they scream and yell. Parents side with their kids who pressure teachers to lower the standards

As an administrator and a teacher, I have had parents come in to argue about their child's grades. To me, the grades were far too generous; to middle-class parents, they were often an affront to their sense of entitlement. If their kids did a mediocre job in class, many parents expected them to obtain at least a B. While teaching in New York and Florida, when I giving C's or D's to bright middle-class kids who have done poor or mediocre work, some parents actually accused me of destroying their children's futures. I told them to look at their own child's work habits and study skills…then come and speak to me.

It is not only parents, however, who are siding with students in their attempts to get out of hard work.

Schools play into this trend too! I've been amazed to see how easy it is for students in public schools to manipulate guidance counselors and administrators to get them out of classes they don't like. They have been sent a message that they don't have to struggle to achieve if things are not perfect. When these students graduate from high school and enter the real world, they are shocked to find that the "bubble" of a world is not a perfect place and cannot cope. Their parents cannot aid them at that point in their lives...for some it is just too late.

I have spoken to numerous college administrators and recruiters that keep complaining that students are coming to them unprepared. Over the past 5 years, I have taught undergraduate classes. I had to "backtrack" and review high school skills before I went on to my syllabus because most of my classes were not prepared at that level. From my viewpoint, I agree that the colleges should be raise admission standards and not accept mediocre students unless cuts have to be made in the budget.

Coming into the teaching, I didn't object to the heightened standards required of educators in the No Child Left Behind law. From what I have been exposed to over the past 20 years, I do not believe our students are learning...they are just studying for the state tests! Yes, there is always room for improvement. Nonetheless, teachers have no control over student ambition and determination, which have to come from the home environment and from each individual student.

I feel that the best lesson that I passed along to all of my students, over the years, was to merely point them in the right direction but it was up to them to become a success!

Chapter 42

FOUNTAIN FOCUS STRATEGIES TO AFFIRM YOUR STUDENTS CONTINUALLY IN THE CLASS

Affirmation is one of a teacher's most effective teaching tools! That's because affirmation is a multi-faceted readiness tool. It readies your students to give an EFFORT in your classroom. It readies them to believe that they can achieve and become successful at what you give them to do in the classroom environment. Also, it readies your students to believe that they fit in and belong and can take their rightful place in the classroom. It readies them to expect to learn…and to LEARN!!!

We have long recognized the need human beings have to be affirmed in the learning process. We have also recognized for a long time how people can be on top of the world one day and feel like they're on the bottom the next. That's why the need to give your students affirmation is CONSTANT! There are many ways that you can affirm your students individually and continuously even though you have a roomful of students.

> *"We all need affirmation at particular times if we are to learn and grow easily and continually."*
> D. L. Fountain

There are various levels of affirmation that you can offer your students. Make no mistake: We tell students how we expect them to behave, perform, and feel about themselves by what we say DIRECTLY to them as well as by what we say ABOUT them. Here are a few powerful messages and positive affirmations that you can deliver to your students easily everyday.

Fountain FOCUS Point #1—First, looking closely at your students within the first couple weeks of school should reveal that your students need a lot of affirmation during this changing period. Time and time again, you should be saying to your students, "You can have power and be strong and still have needs," "You don't have to get angry and act out to get attention or to be taken care of," and "It's normal and healthy to start differentiating feelings and actions as well as to ask that your needs be met."

Fountain FOCUS Point #2—Second, as your students get ready to do things their own way, their need for affirmation does not diminish. That's why you, the teachers, will move your students to greater heights when you tell them, "You should THINK before you adopt an opinion or belief as your own," "You can TRUST your feelings to help you decide," and "It is okay to disagree." Students need to be told, " I really like seeing that you are working and trying new things in order to improve yourself. After all, this is one of the things that getting an education and being a self-sustaining person are all about."

Fountain FOCUS #3—Third, when your students are starting to self-actualize is a very important time. We all have strong needs for affirmation at such times. You provide very powerful affirmation when you state to your students that it is okay to try things, change things, and even think things-they will have your support and protection when they do...Every time you say to your students, "I'm so glad to see you do something," you are giving vital affirmation for self-actualizing and initiating action.

STUDENTS ALWAYS NEED
AFFIRMATION
WHEN THEY BEGIN TO DO
CAUSE-AND-EFFECT
THINKING

Fountain FOCUS Point #4—Fourth, all people really need affirmation when they begin to do cause-and-effect thinking-which begins even before preschool for children. You need to remind your students that they can REFLECT and SENSE at the same time. You need to say, "I'm glad to see you budding into an intelligent individual." You can say, "You don't have to be concerned about me when you think-just think", and "I'm glad you're here trying diverse interests", and "I want and expect you to continually learn about cause-and-effect thinking."

Fountain FOCUS Point #5—Fifth, we all need affirmation as we work through old problems and new ones. Your students need affirmation as they separate from relationships with parents, siblings, and others. You can say, "It is good to know who you are-and be who you are." And, of course, when you say "I like you", or "I respect what you have become", you affirm in a complete and nurturing kind of way. Your students need to be told that you see them recycling, going over old needs and problems, and facing new ones. Your class needs to know that it is okay to work through and separate as well as assume responsibility for their own needs, feelings, and behaviors as grown-up people in this world.

FOUNTAIN FOCUS

M O T I V A T I O N ! ! ! ! !

- There are many ways to actually affirm students in your classroom without saying a word.
- A nod or a smile can make a student feel more confident as well as more successful.
- Other nonverbal gestures can make students feel smarter, more confident-and want to work harder in your classroom.
- It is wise to identify all the nonverbal gestures you can use to affirm every student in class as frequently as possible.

THE FOUNTAIN FOCUS:
WHATEVER WORKS!

- Remember, Fountain FOCUS affirmation plays a "GIANT ROLE" in individual motivation!!

- If you want students to be more motivated in your classroom, you ought to make sure you give them the same things you want as educators.

- Your students want appreciation for being who they are and what they are doing in your class.

- Your class wants to feel "in" and be "in on" things that go on in your room.

- Your students want a sensitive and compassionate teacher regarding their problems.

- If you assume this Fountain FOCUS role in your classroom, you may find that you will be much more influential when motivating your students regardless of the situation!!!

Chapter 43

WHEN STUDENTS DECIDE...

Since time began, adults have worried about the choices young people make. And our concern is intensified because young people have more choices to make in this modern world-and more freedom to choose. In addition, there are more forces trying to influence the decisions young people make today. Unfortunately, many young people are in life situations that force them to make choices alone.

We all know that good decisions will help young people be successful-and that bad ones can hurt them, so our concerns about the choices that our students make are valid. It would be nice if you could just tell the students in your class how and what to choose. But telling won't work! It never has worked, and it never will.

> First, you must understand that your students often don't have enough knowledge and experience to know what options are available to them. Your students don't always see their choices because they don't want to. These are the reasons why you must help the students in your classroom identify the options and alternatives they have to choose from.
>
> Second, you need to point out both the advantages and the disadvantages of each option. In the process, you must hear what the students have to say about the advantages and the disadvantages you offer to them. And if you think an option has advantages but your students do not, it is really not a viable option unless we can do something convincing.

Third, you must help your students see the consequences in each choice. To do so effectively, you must understand that a consequence is a result of an action that can be positive, negative, or neutral. You often do a good job of explaining the negative consequences, but, sometimes, don't do as well using positive consequences to influence your students. Yet, utilizing the positive outcome of studying, coming to school, and working hard must be part of your action throughout the day.

Finally, you should ask yourself a very important question: What is it about the things students choose that is worthy of their choice? If you do not ask this question, you may never understand the situation well enough to advise your students wisely and be influential.

On the other hand, you may be surprised at both the understanding and learning you acquire from answering this question-and also be surprised how often your advice offers nothing in the student's eyes when you fail to consider this question. In fact, you may find the choices you are suggesting are good for you, but not so great for your students. When this is the case, you must make adjustments or the choices you are recommending are not likely to be followed.

FOUNTAIN FOCUS DISCIPLINE TIPS

FOCUS 1 * Be aware that the only way some students are able to establish a friendship is by telling someone all they know. Their past experiences have proven to them that this is true. The problem is accentuated because they must continually search for more information to tell someone. Use empathy, sympathy, and corrective counseling. Deal privately in an open, honest, and caring way. In the process, see that the student gets attention for positive behavior. Then she or he will be better able to stop the habit. (Does this remind you of someone in your class?)

FOCUS 2* When you are counseling your students and trying to get them to move in specific directions, it is often effective to add the "conditional strategy" to your advice. Making your advice conditional can be motivational-and actually produce easier acceptance. Say to your students, "I am asking you to give this idea a try. Just start and see how it goes. If you continue to have problems, I will come up with another idea for you." Try this conditional approach occasionally. It works-especially when you are sure that your student's effort will produce results. (Has anyone come used this strategy with their class?)

FOCUS 3* Think twice before posing a question to a non-listener in order to gain his or her attention. This technique only makes everyone in the class aware that someone isn't giving their full attention to what you are doing. Too, the questioned student may laugh or counter with some other silly or defensive reaction that instills a negative climate in your classroom. For best results, walk toward the student's desk and station yourself close to him or her as you teach. Then, counsel him or her quietly and privately at a later time, and if it persists, bring in the parents and principal for the counseling session.

FOUNTAIN FOCUS POINTS TO PONDER:

1. Why is it imperative that you listen to your students' views concerning the advantages and the disadvantages of different alternatives??

2. What actions can you take to help your students identify the consequences that may accompany the choices they make??

3. In what ways does your behavior in your classroom reflect student-centered choices??

Chapter 44

FOUNTAIN FOCUS

DISCIPLINE AND NEEDS ASSESSMENT

Problems and Needs Regarding Discipline Problems

Please indicate the extent to which the following are problems for you
1 – Never Occurs 2 – Sometimes Occurs 3 – Occurs Often 4 – Occurs Frequently

______ 1. Disruptive behavior
______ 2. Deciding whether I should call certain behaviors discipline problems versus letting a behavior "slide"
______ 3. Withdrawn students
______ 4. Winning over students' feelings
______ 5. Sarcastic nonverbal reactions from students
______ 6. Getting the lessons done on a time schedule
______ 7. Getting students to participate in the lesson
______ 8. Cursing by the students
______ 9. Deciding the best seating arrangements
______10. Bathroom going and a proper bathroom policy
______11. Homework not being done
______12. Marking all the homeworks handed in
______13. Late homework
______14. My homework policy in general
______15. Latecomers
______16. Calling out
______17. Class clowns
______18. Handing out papers and materials

______19. Students talking to each other during the lesson
______20. Cheating
______21. Fighting among students
______22. Verbal "put-downs" among students
______23. Verbal wisecracks at me
______24. Students throwing things
______25. Students who wear hats
______26. Students with "MP3 players or iPods" (personal stereos)
______27. Students with beepers
______28. Students with weapons
______29. Students who are high
______30. students who carry drugs
______31. Students who are dealing drugs
______32. Keeping students motivated
______33. Parents coming into my class
______34. Confrontational students
______35. Students getting out of their seats
______36. Feeling better related to the students
______37, Losing my patience
______38. Some of my procedures (like: ______________________________,
______________________________, ______________________________)
______39. Lack of equipment and materials (like: ______________________,
______________________________, ______________________________)
______40. Deciding whether to confront a student during class or let it slide until after class, or just to overlook the behavior
______41. Being completely honest with myself and the class about the subject matter
______42. Being honest about all rules
______43. Being honest in general interactions with the students
______44. Following through on any warnings
______45. Getting support from the administration on my rewards and punishments
______46. Being accused of being unfair
______47. Not believing in the whole curriculum in teaching
______48. Putting emotions into some of my lessons
______49. Making my lessons relate to students'experiences
______50. Getting the students to interact with each other, besides me
______51. Helping the students feel a sense of direction and the goal of the lesson
______52. Explaining everything very well
______53. Handling students' anger

______54. Disturbances right outside my classroom
______55. My rules falling apart
______56. Handling the "See me after class!"
______57. Deciding the proper rewards and punishments
______58. Asserting myself
______59. Students when I'm substituting or doing a coverage
______60. Designing good "do-nows" or short worksheets
______61. I feel as though I'm alone with these problems.
______62. I feel frustrated in my efforts about handling "discipline problems"
______63. I feel the problem is always the students
______64. I feel the problem is the administration
______65. I feel the problem is the parents and home life
______66. I feel the problem is the students' peers
______67. I feel the problem is none of these
______68. I feel the problem is sometimes my own personal style
______69. I feel the problem is the environment of my classroom
______70. I feel the problem is sometimes in procedures
______71. I feel the problem is in the delivery of my lessons
______72. Other:____

Chapter 45

FOUNTAIN FOCUS

NEW TEACHER SURVEY

This is a measurement survey for new and beginning teachers. It is a fact that often the average new teacher goes through almost five years of trial and error trying to learn how to manage a class to best eliminate many discipline problems. Some teachers, during this time, just give up and quit teaching. Among these teachers are often potentially good teachers, people who really care about students, but, due to the stress in this area of the job, just give up. It shouldn't take five years to better manage disruptive behavior, and we shouldn't lose these caring, ill-prepared teachers. By answering the questions below, you will be helped to find out where your weaknesses, and pitfalls may be beforehand. This can save you from a lot of pointless years of distress, save many conscientious and responsible student learning from many disruptions, and aid all of us to keep you as a compassionate and valuable teacher.

1. I think that if I am myself, and often very honest with the class, that this openness with my class can often cause discipline problems.

2. I should try to do and say what other good teachers have said and done.

3. Almost always, if I feel disrupted by a student, I should not let that behavior slide.

4. I should “go after” students who withdraw, e.g. fall asleep in my class.
5. It’s important for me, in order to be a good teacher, to try to always “win” students’ feelings, not just get their correct behavior,so that they have the correct feelings about school

6. If a student from outside my class is disrupting my class by waving at one of my students through the classroom door window, I should first “go after” the student outside my door.

7. It’s best to have my class sit in rows, rather than in a circle.

8. It’s fine if I usually don’t express emotions in my class; it’s better if I’m mostly cognitive, and get across the ideas presented in the lesson.

9. It’s always important that I have everyone’s attention.

10. It’s very important that I stop students’ digressions and “off-the-lesson questions” in order that I get my lesson plan done.

11. Exercising control in almost all situations is very important.

12. I shouldn’t really be “myself” with a class. Instead, I should try to be the “teacher.”

13. Keeping track of things is not so important as being able to explain abstract ideas.

14. It’s okay if I don’t believe in all of the curriculum that I’m teaching, as long as I can convince my students to study the material.

15. It’s best if I can often go from the curriculum, then to examples of how the curriculum relates to students’ lives.

16. It’s better if the students (in the lesson) interact with me (the teacher) than each other.

17. I know some good rules that I can implement used by a good teacher I once had.

18. I remember some effective lectures to give students who violate my rules (that my past teachers used to give me).

19. I have no problem calling a parent the second a child violates one of my rules.

20. If I am reprimanding a student, and the student says: "I won't do it, big deal!" I should know how to give the next punishment (for such an attitude).

21. I know how to reprimand students who call out.

22. I know how to go after students during a test who are cheating.

23. It's important for me to not smile or laugh when a student in my class is being funny as a " class clown."

24. I know how to break up a fight between two students by myself.

25. I know how to speak warmly to a student who might have a crush on me.

26. If I'm a substitute teacher, I can usually follow the lesson left for me by the regular teacher.

It's OK for me to let elementary school students rely on their parents somewhat to help them enter the class in the morning (hang up their coats, turn in their homework, read the problem of the day, etc.) since it will help them and me to have them ready for work in the morning.

CHAPTER 46

KEEP THIS IN MIND

FOCUS A—Before you ever meet your students you should talk with the principal or the person in charge of discipline at your school. Every school has its own policies and new teachers must know them inside out to avoid catastrophe down the road. Also talk to teachers to find out what happens to students when they are sent out of the room. If sending them down to the office is a reward for them, then by all means, keep them with you (within reason of course).

FOCUS B—Make a list of general policies. These are not rules. Policies are the concepts that you base your classroom on. Just think about the absolutes. What are the issues that absolutely must (or must not) occur in order for you to teach your students? Policies are issues that cannot be compromised. Example: Students will feel comfortable and safe in class.

FOCUS C—Make your class rules. Have your policies in front of you when you do this. Try and anticipate your pet peeves. If there are certain areas of the room that students should not have access to (your desk or computer) they need to know that up front. Also be ready to make changes when you realize that a rule doesn't work out. From the policy example above, I have a rule that students can not laugh at another when he/she stumbles on words while reading out loud. (You might think about handing out the policies on the first day to your students and see what rules they come up with. You might be surprised on how well they do!)

FOCUS D—The Delivery. How you present yourself on the first day of school is of the up most importance. All teachers will agree with me here.

Where teachers disagree, is what "side" of the teacher the students should see. You've heard the old saying, "Don't smile before Thanksgiving!"? I don't necessarily agree with this however, I prefer to be all business. Some call this old fashioned mean. The first day is when the tone is set in the classroom. The first day will be about the scariest event you'll go through, however, be sure to be thinking straight. Prepare...Prepare...Prepare. This may sound a bit strange, but even though it is the day for introductions and policies, you must know what you will say when you stand in front of your class for the first time. Do NOT "wing-it." I wrote down word for word what I wanted to say and thought through the words over and over in my head. In addition to letting students know that you WILL have control of the class, this is also the time to let them know that you do look forward to getting to know them and that you do care for them. It truly is possible for these "two sides" to both show themselves in the same class period!

FOCUS E—I like to take attendance using only last names; it is more like boot camp that way. I am especially hard on the freshman. I do not want them to start off high school thinking they can just coast along. I encourage them to do great things with the new start that they have. I have students take turns reading the rules out loud and I discuss them carefully and in great detail. I then spend time (once again, more with the freshman) on the discipline system of our school. Here is where I like to shake students up.

FOCUS F—Our school discipline system is based on points. Students get discipline points for acting up in class, tardies etc.. At 10 and/or 15 points, a letter goes home to the parents or I make a phone call. At 20 points the student is dropped from the class for the semester with an F, affectionately known as the "WF" for Withdraw with an F. Many freshman do not understand that teachers really can/will do this. I tell students on the first day of school that the sacrificial lamb may step forward because many times it takes one to be kicked out for the rest to believe. As far as I am concerned, the faster we get that over with, the faster I will have a class that I can enjoy teaching!

FOCUS G—I know that elementary teachers spend a lot of time doing this. However, I think its importance is overlooked many times on the secondary level. This is a mistake. Students must know YOUR definition of what good behavior is. Let them know exactly how you want things done, for example: when is it ok to sharpen a pencil, how do students get work when absent, when is a good time to ask about grades. It is also a good idea to let students know what "sets you off." For me it is a crowd around my desk at the beginning of the hour. I tell them up front that I don't like it and students seem to understand. As a new teacher knowing good procedures is not easy. It takes time to know what things students won't know how to do without instructions.

FOCUS H—Once again, this tough attitude can coincide with the caring and enthusiastic attitude. Within the first week of class, I like to find time to read, Don't Eat The Teacher! Yes, I have taught elementary school through college level! Some students do roll their eyes, but all listen and most enjoy! The message in this children's book is a good one for the beginning of the school year. It speaks of being able to do what you want to do if you set your mind to it, but understanding that times can be lonely and confusing also. I also read this book to students at the end of the year as a farewell -graduation -from-my- class- wish.

Chapter 47

WHAT IS A TEACHER GUIDE?

Created while directing the ACP program on college campus:

"Teacher-Guiding" is the establishment of a personal relationship for the purpose of professional instruction and assistance. In education, the value of guiding or mentoring has been recognized in the use of teachers and other professionals in one-on-one instruction of students. Teacher-Guiding or Teacher-Mentoring programs have been implemented recently for beginning teacher induction and continuing staff development.

WHAT ARE THE CHARACTERISTICS AND ACTIVITIES OF MENTORING?

From the literature on mentoring in professions, D. L. Fountain has compiled a list of ten characteristics inherent in any mentor-protégé relationship.

1. Teacher-Guide (mentor-protégé) relationships grow out of voluntary interaction.

2. The Teacher-Guide relationship has a life cycle: introduction; mutual trust-building; teaching of risk-taking, communication, and professional skills; transfer of professional standards; and dissolution.

3. People become mentors to pass down information to the next generation.

4. Content Area Guides encourage teachers in setting and attaining short- and long-term goals.

5. Education professors direct technically and professionally. Teacher-Guides teach their beginners skills necessary to survive daily experiences and promote career-scope professional development.

6. Guides protect teachers from major mistakes by limiting their exposure to responsibility.

7. Guides provide opportunities for the teacher to observe and participate in their work.

8. Guides ARE role models.

9. Guides sponsor their teachers organizationally and professionally.

10. "Teacher-Guide Relationships" end, amiably or bitterly.

HONORING A TRADITIONAL PROGRESSION:

Some school systems have formalized mentoring processes as part of newly developed induction programs, thus compromising some of the mentor-protégé relationship characteristics. Voluntary participation becomes mandatory for the protégé. At the same time the sphere of influences in which the mentor would ordinarily affect the protégé is decreased by time and authority restrictions. The mentor cannot regulate the beginning teacher's levels of responsibility. The mentor does not have the freedom to direct the protégé's activities nor the time to adequately oversee developing classroom performance. Creating a school environment, which openly offers assistance and provides the means to expand the initiate's repertoire of teaching techniques and classroom management skills, can support the mentoring relationship.

As an interactive system, mentoring benefits all participants: the mentor, the protege, and the school system. Mentors gain the satisfaction of being able to transfer skills and knowledge accumulated through extensive professional practice. Much of this knowledge is intangible and is not contained in teacher preparation programs. It might be lost entirely if it were not rediscovered by each beginner. The questions from beginning teachers provide opportunities for mentor teachers to reexamine their own classroom practices and the effects of accepted instructional techniques on the teaching/learning process.

The protégé benefits in three major ways: fast assimilation into the school environment, establishment of professional competence, and introduction to teaching as a continually developing, lifelong career. One of the most recognized uses of mentoring is the conveyance of operating procedures to the beginner

The school administration provides an introduction to the rules but the mentor teaches the skills necessary to comply and cope with them The mentor provides the protégé with opportunities to develop professional competence through a cycle of observation/assessment/practice/assessment. This permits continuous communication and constant feedback to the protégé. Classroom skills develop under the mentor's constant and consistent assistance. The mentor also guides the protégé though the maze of local and state administration systems, which potentially influence the practices of the classroom teacher. Finally, the mentor directs the protégé to professional organizations for academic and professional development.

The school district benefits both directly and indirectly from mentoring programs. A school, which enthusiastically welcomes beginning teachers and initiates them to active participation in the educational processes potentially reduces its teacher attrition rate Furthermore, close supervision of the beginning teacher catches problems, which may affect the instructional process or discourage the teacher. Involving experienced teachers in the program and providing them the opportunity to pass on their expertise further demonstrates long-term professional interest in the faculty and provides an environment conducive to lifelong professional careers.

Confusing "assessment" with "evaluation" provides a common cause of Teacher-Guide program failure An effective mentoring process is built on a foundation of mutual trust. The objective of the process is assistance. Both trust and assistance are placed in serious jeopardy if the mentor is saddled with evaluation responsibilities. Assessment, however, is an important part of the mentoring process, which allows the protege self-criticism and direction for improvement Programs can resolve this conflict by appointing separate evaluators who meet with the protege, and mentor to discuss performance evaluations.

Mandatory program participation could cause problems in the mentoring process, but surveys of post-program protégés and mentors repeatedly report enthusiastic support of organized mentoring programs This seems to indicate that schools can establish an environment for effective mentoring in mandatory programs.

Using a Teacher-Guide program to fulfill state-mandated and district-required certification, induction, and staff development programs loads mentoring with obligations that the technique is not designed to handle. The Teacher-Guide is a direct link to the profession, not a stand-in for administration

In most teacher mentoring programs, mentoring forms a basic component of a multipurpose teacher induction program. Many induction programs seek to qualify a new teacher for certification and permanent employment, necessitating evaluation of teaching skills and providing programs to improve those skills to preset standards. The literature provides many examples of these mentoring-evaluation program hybrids. Another purpose for supporting the teacher mentor/protégé relationship with additional induction activities is to restore some of the benefits of professional mentoring which are necessarily curtailed by the teaching environment: time constraints and limitations of personnel interaction. The Fountain FOCUS Committee discussed the problems common to the adaptation of the traditionally idealistic relationship of Teacher-Guide or Mentor and Protégé to the teacher's real world of limited time and structured activities.

The multipurpose programs come in two varieties: those using mentoring as a part of an induction process and those using mentoring as a tool for general staff development. This "Advisory/Assessment Team" consists of a school administrator, an instructional consultant and a peer teacher who acts as a mentor to the beginner. These programs back up both the mentor and the protégé with separate supporting activities. The system has received favorable reviews, despite the misleading use of the term "assessment": the final team "assessment" determines the employment status for the protégé.

Our ACP program offers to bring professionalism the mentoring process by training senior teachers as master teachers to instruct beginning and experienced teachers in advanced instructional techniques and classroom skills. Each trained "mentor" is assigned a group of "protégés." The mentor also is responsible for curriculum development and the exploration of new instructional techniques. The concept of training experienced teachers to advise and monitor a group of other teachers does not evolve from developments in the use of mentoring as much as it is derived from twenty years of induction program development.

The success of mentoring programs has been documented largely by opinion survey. Most of the programs using teacher mentoring are less than four years old. Long-term objectives, including the retention of new teachers and development of experienced ones, have had insufficient time to be realized. However, surveys of perceptions of program success overwhelmingly conclude that beginning teachers expand their techniques, improve teaching skills, and learn classroom management Furthermore, mentors do appreciate the opportunity to and do pass their expertise on to new teachers. The varieties of mentoring programs described in the literature should allow any school district to find a model, which fits its budget, time, and spatial constraints.

MORE "TEACHER-GUIDING" TO COME IN MY FUTURE BOOKS...

Appendix A

CHARACTERISTICS OF EFFECTIVE PROGRAMS

Several authors have proposed models for effective alternative certification programs. One of the leading authorities on the subject, D. L. Fountain suggests a six-point model that begins by being market driven. By this, she means that programs should be designed specifically to meet the needs of particular regions or subject areas. These needs include, for example, shortages in urban and rural areas, and in subjects such as math, science, and special education. An effective ACP program should also be tailored to meet the specific needs of the participants; for example, taking into account the educational backgrounds and learning styles of older teacher candidates. Good AC programs should prepare individuals for specific positions in specific schools, and should place participants in those positions early in the training. Also, prospective teachers should have mentors and should go through their training in cohorts so that they will have sufficient support. Finally, research suggests that effective ACP programs work as collaborative efforts between state departments of education, colleges and universities, and local school districts.

Other suggestions for quality ACP programs include rigorous screening, high-quality pre-service training in pedagogy, classroom management, and human development. In addition, there needs to be a highly structured, well-supervised induction period that includes close supervision and guidance by an experienced teacher for at least one year, plus ongoing professional development and post-internship training.

While I was the Director of the Alternative Certification Program in Houston, our evaluation team outlined 10 suggestions that they received from teacher advisors who had supervised ACP interns. While not an outline of an effective program, these items touch on several themes that emerged from the review and research literature discussed above. They include the following ten guides:

1. Provide ACP interns with more on-the-job classroom experience prior to being assigned as teacher of record.

2. Continue training in classroom management and discipline after the intern becomes the teacher of record.

3. Provide opportunities for interns to observe other veteran teachers in the classroom.

4. Give supervising teachers more training for their role in the program.

5. Continue the opportunity for teacher advisors to work with the interns in small groups.

6. Provide more information about classroom management as applied to groups of students.

7. Provide more information about the principles of learning.

8. Assist the intern to become more active as a helper or aid when assigned to the supervising teacher's class.

9. Provide more information about child development.

10. Start interns' training at the beginning of the summer.

Common themes that emerge from the research on effective alternative certification programs FOCUS on six points:

1. High standards and proper screening of candidates for entry into ACP programs.

2. Solid academic instruction in pedagogy, subject matter, classroom management, and child development—preferably before the teacher candidate begins to teach.

3. An organized and comprehensive system of support from experienced, trained mentors once the candidate begins working in a school.

4. If possible, a period of observation and assistance in the classroom by an experienced teacher before the candidate begins teaching solo.

5. Ongoing training, instruction, and reflection once the candidate assumes control of a classroom.

6. Continuous monitoring, evaluation, and feedback of individual and group performance to allow for adjustment and improvement in teaching and program management.

Some skeptics of ACP programs have suggested that ACP teachers should be expected to pass all certification exams required for standard certification before taking over a classroom of students on their own. But, I believe that our ACP candidates learn so much in their classrooms before gaining full certification.

The research and lessons learned regarding ACP programs could have implications for college-based programs. Many if not all of the above criteria that contribute to the effectiveness of ACP programs can be applied to undergraduate teacher-education programs. As this area of research moves forward, researchers and practitioners in all teacher preparation programs need to stay informed about new findings and consider the implications for their individual certification programs.

Appendix B

WHAT IS YOUR CLASSROOM DISCIPLINE APPROACH?

Respond to these 15 questions and learn more about your classroom discipline approach. The directions are very easy to understand.

- Read each statement carefully.
- Write your answer on the given line from the scale below.
- Respond to the statement based upon either actual or imagined experience.
- Follow the scoring directions below.

5 points = **Strongly Agree**
4 points = **Agree**
3 points = **Neutral**
2 points = **Disagree**
1 points = **Strongly Disagree**

1. If a student is disruptive during class, I assign her/him to detention, without further discussion. _____

2. I do not want to impose any rules on my students. _____

3. The classroom must be quiet in order for my students to learn. _____

4. I am concerned about both what my students learn and how they learn it. _____

5. If a student turns in late homework, it is not my problem. _____

6. I do not want to reprimand a student because it might hurt her/his feelings. _____

7. Classroom preparation is not worth my effort. _____

8. I always try to explain the reasons behind my decisions and rules. _____

9. I will not accept excuses from a student who is tardy. _____

10. The emotional well being of my students is more important than classroom control. _____

11. My students understand that they can interrupt my lecture if they have a relevant question. _____

12. If a student requests a hall pass, I always honor the request. _____

13. The classroom is always bustling with students working on their projects or performing exploratory activities in groups. _____

14. I always make sure to let the students show ownership in their classroom. _____

15. My students know not to ask to go outside of the classroom if I am instructing. _____

TO SCORE YOUR CLASSROOM DISCIPLINE APPROACH:

Add your responses to statements 1, 3, 9, and 15.
This is the Authoritarian Approach.

Add your responses to 4, 8, 11, and 14.
This is the Authoritative Approach.

Add your responses to 6, 10, 12, and 13.
This is the Laissez Faire Approach.

Add your responses to 2, 5, and 7.
This is the Apathetic Approach.

√ The result is your Classroom Discipline Approach profile. Your score for each discipline approach can range from 3-20. A high score indicates a strong preference for that particular Discipline Approach.

√ After you have scored your quiz, and determined your discipline approach, read the descriptions of each discipline approach. You may see a little bit of yourself in each one...I know that I have over the past 20 years in education.

√ As you gain teaching experience, you may find that your preferred discipline approach will change. Over time, your discipline approach may become more diverse or more FOCUSED!

√ It may be suitable to rely upon a specific discipline approach when addressing a particular situation or subject. Perhaps the successful teacher is the one who can evaluate a situation and then apply the appropriate discipline approach.

√ Finally, remember that the intent of this exercise is to inform you and arouse your curiosity regarding classroom discipline approaches.

Appendix C

TEACHING...MY PRIVILEGE [FOR ALL OF MRS. FOUNTAIN'S KIDS!!]

I did not know that my college degrees
would be of little consolation when facing
a classroom of students, older and young.
I did not know that ten minutes could seem
like ten hours when there is "Idle Time"
and an eight-hour school day was far too
short for a well-planned day of teaching.
I did not know that a single "Yes Ma'am"
from a disrespectful child would make me
feel like I am on TOP OF THE WORLD.
I did not know that the sound of children's
laughter could drown out the sound of the
world's cruelness and sadness.
I did not know I would become a scavenger
and teaching materials would feel like gold.
I did not know that after many, many years
of teaching, I would feel so much wiser,
spry, frazzled, and happier, all at once...
I will never state that TEACHING was just
my job but it will always be MY PRIVILEGE!

D. L. Fountain

Appendix D

17 COMMANDMENTS

(…FOR MY COLLEAGUES IN THE TRENCHES…YOU ARE THE BEST!)

Teach them to read.
Teach them to love to learn.
Teach them where to find information.
Teach them to truly listen.
Teach them to enunciate and communicate.
Teach them to respect inventiveness.
Teach them to be thankful for surrounding beauty.
Teach them not to obliterate but savor.
Teach them how to decipher problems.
Teach them how to deal with disappointment.
Teach them to learn from the past.
Teach them to enjoy the present.
Teach them to prepare for the future.
Teach them to appreciate differences.
Teach them how to create and innovate.
Teach them how to cooperate and be positive.
Teach them how to instruct and raise
their own children someday…

D. L. Fountain

Appendix E

OTHER WAYS TO SAY "VERY GOOD"

WHEN YOU CAN'T THINK OF WHAT TO SAY…ON CERTAIN DAYS IN YOUR CLASSROOM

You're on the right track now!
You've got it made.
SUPER!
That's right!That's good.
You're really working hard today.

You are very good at that.
That's coming along nicely.
GOOD WORK! I'm happy to see you working like that.
That's much, much better!
Exactly right.
I'm proud of the way you worked today.
You're doing that much better today.
You've just about got it.
That's the best you've ever done.
You're doing a good job.
THAT'S IT!
Now you've figured it out.
That's quite an improvement.
GREAT! I knew you could do it.
Congratulations!
Not bad.
Keep working on it.
You're improving.
Now you have it!
You are learning fast.
Good for you!
Couldn't have done it better myself.
Aren't you proud of yourself?
One more time and you'll have it.
You really make my job fun.
That's the right way to do it.
You're getting better every day.
That's the best ever.
You've just about mastered it.
PERFECT! That's better than ever.
Much better!
WONDERFUL!
You must have been practicing.
You did that very well.
FINE!
Nice going.
You're really going to town.
OUTSTANDING!

FANTASTIC!
TREMENDOUS!
That's how to handle that.
Now that's what I call a fine job.That's great.
Right on!
You're really improving.
You're doing beautifully!
SUPERB!
Good remembering.
You've got that down pat.
You certainly did well today.
Keep it up!
Congratulations. You got it right!
You did a lot of work today.
Well look at you go.
That's it.
I'm very proud of you.
MARVELOUS! I like that.
Way to go!
Now you have the hang of it.
You're doing fine! Good thinking.
You are really learning a lot.
Good going.
I've never seen anyone do it better.
Keep on trying.
You outdid yourself today!
Good for you!
I think you've got it now.
That's a good (boy/girl).
Good job, (person's name).
You figured that out fast.
You remembered!
That's really nice.
That kind of work makes me happy.
It's such a pleasure to teach when you work like that!
I think you're doing the right thing.
That's the way to get it done!
You are sensational!

You have your brain gear on!
That is better that the first time!
First class work!
Excellent effort!
You are going to the top!
Nothing can stop you now!
Keep up the wonderful effort!
That's the way, ah uh, i like it, ah uh!
Nice going!
You are really staying on task today!
That is not bad at all!
Wow, are you good!
You did it that time!
You do not miss anything!!

Printed in the United States
57929LVS00005B/208

9 781424 123766